Flack Fairy

Flack Fairy

Navigating PR and Media for Venture-Backed Startups

Beck Bamberger, PhD

◁ **BAD IDEAS GROUP**

FLACK FAIRY
Navigating PR and Media for Venture-Backed Startups

FIRST EDITION

ISBN   978-1-5445-4742-8   *Hardcover*
       978-1-5445-4741-1   *Paperback*
       978-1-5445-4743-5   *Ebook*
       978-1-5445-4744-2   *Audiobook*

Contents

Glossary

- **Cap table:** The table or spreadsheet showcasing who owns what at your startup.
- **Competitive moat:** This so-called moat, popularized by Warren Buffett as an "economic moat," pertains to a startup's ability to keep a competitive edge. I like to think that the deeper your moat, the harder it is to attack your castle.
- **Domain authority:** This is the internet's "score" of how credible a website is relevant to a subject area or industry. It was created by Moz, an SEO company founded back in the early 2000s. Link quality and quantity help boost domain authority, which helps your website outrank those of your competitors.
- **Embargo:** A deal between you, your company, or your publicist and a media person about when certain information can be made public. For instance, a media outlet can "agree to an embargo" and not publish news until a specific time.
- **Exclusive:** A story that is pitched to *one* media outlet or journalist. Public relations people get into big trouble when, for instance, they pitch an exclusive to multiple people at a time. That's a surefire way to ruin a media outlet's trust.

- **Flack Fairy:** A public relations pro who is invisible and magical. I made up this term as a counter illustration to Unicorn (see below).
- **FOMO:** Fear of missing out; usually refers to the anxiety extroverts get when they aren't present at something. However, venture capitalists are subject to FOMO as well regarding hot startups and whether or not they can get on the cap table.
- **ICP:** Ideal customer profile, a term commonly used in marketing.
- **Investor relations:** Communications related specifically to investors, which may have regulatory or legal considerations and constraints.
- **Law of Conservation of Complexity, or Tesler's law:** A theory stating that all systems have an inherent amount of complexity you can't get rid of. The question is, who has to deal with it?
- **LPs:** Limited partners; the individual people, institutions, endowments, family offices, and more that invest in venture capitalists and want to see their money returned. These are the bosses of venture capitalists, rather like how venture capitalists are the bosses of founders. Remember that everyone has a boss.
- **Media relations:** Communications related specifically to media, which typically include reporters, editors, freelancers, bloggers, and more. "Media relations" is often considered a subset of "public relations," but the terms can be used interchangeably. See "public relations" below.
- **Newsjacking:** A tool used by publicists to secure media coverage in the midst of breaking news.
- **Off the record:** An agreement between you and a reporter to ensure your comments or statements will not be attributed to you at all. Explicit confirmation needs to be granted before you can be confident a conversation is off the record.

- **On background:** Similar to being off the record, an agreement between you and a reporter. In this case, your direct comments or statements may be used but will not be attributed to you.
- **On the record:** Anything you say to a reporter may be attributed to you. By default, all conversations with the media should be considered on the record.
- **Platform teams:** Within venture capital funds, the people who support portfolio companies with hiring, business development, community, research, public relations, and more.
- **PR crisis:** A situation that could harm your startup's reputation, such as layoffs, a product outage, or online backlash due to a social media post, and requires immediate attention.
- **Press release:** A formal announcement detailing the news of an organization. It includes a date, headline, quotes, contact information of the company or media person, and more.
- **Public relations (PR):** The catchall term for the various channels for and ways of communicating to stakeholders. Public relations usually includes earned, owned, and paid media.
- **RACI matrix:** A project management framework that will save your life as you hire more people. RACI stands for responsible, accountable, consulted, and informed and is filled out with people's names so everyone knows their roles in a project, such as hiring a public relations agency.
- **Stakeholders:** The various people your startup impacts. These often include investors, employees, board members, customers, vendors, regulatory bodies, communities your product or service touches, and more.
- **Top-tier media:** Usually national media outlets rather than media outlets that cover local news or niche industries.
- **Unicorn:** A venture-backed startup valued at more than $1 billion. Aileen Lee created the term back in the 2010s, when unicorns were quite rare in the venture space.

- **VC:** Venture capitalist; someone who invests in startups and hopes to make obscene returns on the capital invested.
- **WIIFM:** "What's in it for me?" Leads, prospective clients, employees, and sometimes anyone you want to nudge into doing something for you needs a WIIFM.

Author's Note

___

While I wrote this book as a "tell-all" for founders building venture-backed startups, you'll soon note that the names of journalists, founders, publicists, and VCs (other than one) aren't included. The reason for this is twofold: First, I didn't want to update this darn book with constant editions as people move fluidly around in the venture capital and media ecosystems. Second, it's unbecoming.

Lastly, I love to write, and everything in here was written by me over the course of four weeks. No AI was used. I do love technology, but PR, particularly for venture-backed startups, is such an odd little niche that a machine likely could not pump out the depths of this obscure content.

Introduction

In one corner of the internet, there's a YouTube clip featuring the late Don Valentine. Don Valentine was the founder of Sequoia Capital, and in the clip, he deadpans, "Many, and maybe even most, of the entrepreneurs who come to talk to us can't tell a story." He's at a podium in a lecture hall somewhere at Stanford's business school, addressing an eager audience. He continues, "Learning to tell a story is critically important because that's how the money works. The money flows as *a function of the stories.*"[1]

The clip is now more than fourteen years old, just about as old as BAM, my PR and marketing agency, which has helped dozens of venture-backed startups grow into unicorns, get acquired, or go public via the power of media relations and marketing. I certainly know, and now have the receipts for, what Don meant. It doesn't matter that I know it though. My "problem" slide for venture-backed founders is this: Most of you don't know the sheer power of PR for venture-backed startups. The irony is that the PR around

---

1   Don Valentine, "The Art of Storytelling Is Incredibly Important," lecture, posted February 16, 2024, by Startup Archive, YouTube, https://www.youtube.com/watch?v=uytKVKf52qo.

the power of PR for venture-backed startups has been crap—go figure.

This book is my "solution," and as much as I'd love to have one tidy slide about it, like in your pitch deck, there's frankly too much you need to know to become dangerous and dominant. First, I want you to be dangerous: dangerous enough that you can dodge the blows and "gotchas" that can happen in the arena of media and public relations. This book contains my expertise as an agency owner but more so my discernment as a CEO and investor who doesn't want you wasting money or time. There are a lot of subpar "professionals" out there in the world of PR and media, and they'd love to get a signed budget from you even though they couldn't tell you what you're actually solving in the world let alone convey this to anyone in the media. Some agency Vice President may insist that you sign a twelve-month contract for your seed-stage startup, and I'm here to tell you to wait until you're at least a Series A and then only sign an engagement with a sixty-day rolling termination, for instance. Some "producer" will try to convince you that you've been selected to appear on some unknown TV show for a "small production fee" of $30,000, and I'm telling you to delete that request immediately. In this book, I'm spilling the beans, tea, or whatever else we're spilling these days because this level of transparency will make you dangerous. I've also included numerous real examples, from press releases to media pitches, because tactics trump theory.

Second, I want you to be dominating, to have such a firm handle on how public relations works and how to deploy PR in the lifespan of your startup that you get to your exit faster. I say "faster" deliberately because our experience and data show that our clients (venture-backed startups) raise more money and exit faster than venture-backed startups not engaging in PR, which will be covered in Chapter 1. Here's my hunch about why: It doesn't matter if you're selling a technical SaaS offering to a CTO in a niche industry or multi-year contracts to federal governments because you're ultimately selling to *someone*. That someone is influenced, whether they admit it or not, by the power of media, storytelling, and branding, as Don explains in that clip. When you have consistent storytelling over the long haul of a startup, awareness compounds.

HOW TO USE THIS BOOK

I suggest reading this book from front to back as themes and terminology build upon one another. That's your first step in becoming what I call a "Flack Fairy": someone dangerous and dominating in PR who floats about making media and stories appear, seemingly from nothing, like magic. I chose "fairy" because we needed another fantastical word to go alongside "unicorn," the term Aileen Lee hatched in 2013 to describe startups valued at more than $1 billion.[2] "Flack" just means publicist, and I like alliteration.

Some of you are thinking, "Now I need to be great at *this* too—this Flack Fairy thing?" I know you're fully occupied building your startup. You have to be because three months is three years in startup time, and time is ticking loud as thunder. But like fundraising, PR is *your* job. A venture capitalist isn't going to meet with your junior account rep, and a producer at CNBC is not going to book them for a live TV segment either. That's because you're the one they want; you're the founder. No one should tell the story or raise the money better than you do. PR is a "founder mode" kind of initiative.

The good news is there are great people to support you in

---

2   Aileen Lee, "Welcome to the Unicorn Club: Learning from Billion-Dollar Startups," *TechCrunch*, November 2, 2013, https://techcrunch.com/2013/11/02/welcome-to-the-unicorn-club/.

becoming a Flack Fairy, much like your team helps you fund-raise to become a unicorn. This book is the solution to becoming dangerous and dominating in the realm of public relations. You don't have to do it, just as you don't have to build a company worth billions of dollars. If you become a Flack Fairy, though, the money, as Don stated, will flow as a function of it. Let's get to it.

Chapter 1

The Power of PR

—————

I like to listen to *How I Built This*, a podcast produced by NPR and hosted by Guy Raz. I've noticed, though I am biased, that an inevitable part of each episode is the part where the entrepreneur says, "And then we got this great article in X media outlet, and that really changed things." I haven't done a qualitative analysis on the six-hundred-plus episodes to know for certain the number of times positive media coverage boosted the ascent of a company's path, but I'm confident it is high. That's what this chapter is about: Why earned media is a powerful tool for venture-backed startups as well as what PR is and the most common reasons why a venture-backed startup considers leveraging it.

First, the good news: Great, consistent PR can absolutely help your startup, if not you, directly. Before I wrote this chapter, a founder who had attended a few of our media events reached out to me. She said the media coverage she had obtained over the last few months—thanks to BAM's events, which allowed her to meet journalists and get positive articles written about her and her startup—helped her secure her visa in the US.[3] I hear this kind of story a few times a year. You may roll your eyes and think, "Really? A few good media hits will help me get into this country?" The answer is yes. The US government views favorable media coverage as a positive component of whether you should be in this country or not.

Maybe you don't need a visa to the US; lucky you. Let's look at some math, then, as it relates to how PR can help your startup. We crunch the numbers at BAM every year with a third-party research company and consistently find the venture-backed startups we worked with raised notably larger rounds of funding, up to 107 percent more, compared to other randomly selected venture-backed startups listed on Crunchbase. (See the appendix for the analysis.) Rounds of funding do not dictate exits, and correlation (between higher rounds of funding and working with BAM) does not imply causation (work with BAM and *then* you'll raise more funds), but at least we're dealing with some numbers instead of what founders have told us over the last ten years, including, "That article *totally* sealed the acquisition!" (That quote is one of my favorites, from a Series D startup that exited to a Fortune 1000.)

The flip side, and further evidence of the power of PR, is how negative media coverage can utterly demolish a startup. Most every founder knows the story of Theranos, the blood-testing company founded by Elizabeth Holmes. Few founders know that one of the reasons Theranos folded was a watershed investigative article published in the The *Wall Street Journal*.[4] Sure, one could argue

---

3   This coveted US visa is called the O-1 visa and is awarded to individuals with "extraordinary ability." Read more on this blog: Derek Sturman, "The Value of Media Coverage in O-1 Visa Applications," *Grossman Young & Hammond* (blog), March 28, 2024, https://www.grossmanyoung.com/blog/publicity-o1-visas/.

4   Kari Paul, "'People Wanted to Believe': Reporter Who exposed Theranos on Elizabeth Holmes' Trial," *The Guardian*, August 29, 2021, https://www.theguardian.com/technology/2021/aug/28/elizabeth-holmes-theranos-trial-john-carreyrou; John Carreyrou, "Hot Startup Theranos Has Struggled with Its Blood-Test Technology," *The Wall Street Journal*, October 16, 2015, https://www.wsj.com/articles/theranos-has-struggled-with-blood-tests-1444881901.

that Theranos and other startups of late, such as WeWork and NFX, were self-imploding disasters regardless of media coverage, but I argue that nothing is more halting than the heavy hand of media, particularly if that hand once put you on its stage and front pages.

In short, the power of PR goes both ways. Great media coverage can push your startup to enviable heights, but negative media coverage can topple you right over. Whether you like it or not, the media is powerful, at least in a country like the US. Further, publicists, the people who deal with the media on your behalf, can be quite powerful as well. We'll get to publicists in later chapters, but for now, let's get to what the difference is between PR and various other forms of storytelling.

PAID, EARNED, AND OWNED MEDIA

From billboards to SMS messages to blog posts to a full feature in *Fortune*, pretty much every form of media falls into one of three categories: paid, earned, or owned. Paid is the easiest to understand. If you pay for it, then it's paid media. Social media ads, the billboards on the 101, affiliate links, and paid influencers all fall into this bucket, as shown in the following Venn diagram. On occasion, we'll get a founder who says, "I want to be in *The New York Times* tomorrow. Can you do that?" I say, "Yep. It will just take a really big check." The benefit of paid media is you can say whatever you want.[5] You have full control over the exact message, visuals, and so on. The problem with paid media is that it is paid, of course, and usually considered less credible to an audience. Countless research dissertations and entire academic departments have shown the "credibility" aspect of advertising

---

5   Subject to the media outlet, of course. We're not going to get into the aspects of free speech or its limitations. That's another book.

to be problematic.[6] Moreover, to keep things clear to consumers, media outlets disclose when something in a publication, whether print, digital, or otherwise, is paid.[7] Check out the upper-right area of the following image to better understand advertising in the "paid" area of media.

How about *earned* media, then? Earned media is what publicists typically devote their time and energy to. We try to convince reporters, journalists, editors, and freelancers that a particular client of ours should be highlighted, quoted, and written about. A media segment devoted to you on CNBC, an article about you in *TechCrunch*, a quote of yours included in Bloomberg, and a podcast you were a guest on all fall into the bucket of earned media. Back to that founder who wants to be in *The New York Times* tomorrow. Another version of that ask is, "I want to be in *The New York Times* eventually. Can you do that?" My answer: "Perhaps." We don't control the media. Now, there are lots of things you can do to enhance your chances of favorable media coverage—these and your ascent to understanding them as a Flack Fairy are what this whole book is about. Earned media is far harder to attain but far more credible to audiences as compared to paid media.

Lastly, there's owned media. Owned media are all the platforms you directly control, such as your LinkedIn page, your blog, your email newsletters, your website, what you post on TikTok, and the like. A press release, which is a formal "news announcement" you write up and put on your blog, is owned media.[8] If you con-

---

6   Here's one dissertation to read if you want to knock yourself out: Raoul Bell et al., "Source Memory for Advertisements: The Role of Advertising Message Credibility," *Memory & Cognition* 49, no. 1 (2021): 32–45, https://doi.org/10.3758/s13421-020-01075-9.

7   Yep, government again. The Federal Communications Commission (FCC) oversees truth in advertising and consumer protections across media.

8   If you pay a portal like PR Newswire or PRWeb to put your press release all over the internet, then that's paid. Many startups we work with don't bother writing press releases because a press release does not guarantee media coverage.

trol it and don't have to pay a third party to say what you want to say, it's likely owned media. Owned media has the advantage of potentially being quick, but like paid media, it's not as credible as earned media. As the following diagram illustrates, the overlap of all three of these realms of media (paid, earned, and owned) contributes to your brand. Don't get caught up right now thinking, "But I don't have millions of dollars to do *all* these areas of media." I hear you, and I'll address that a bit later.

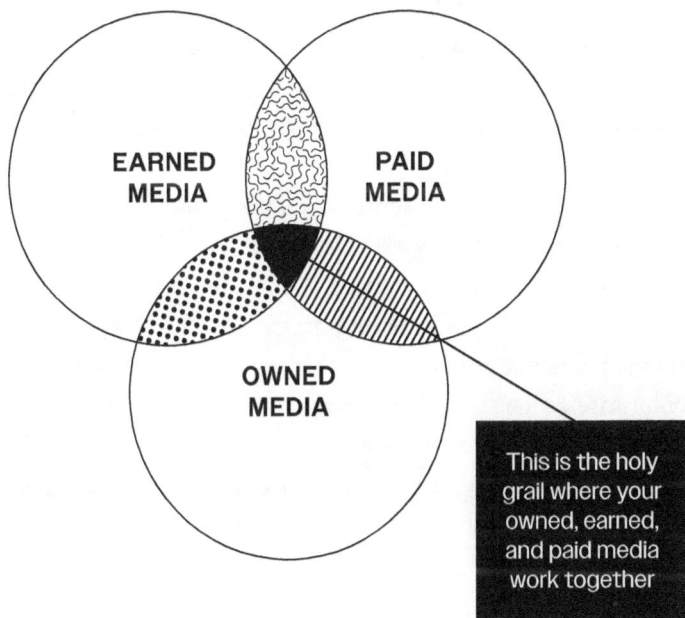

EARNED
MEDIA

PAID
MEDIA

OWNED
MEDIA

This is the holy grail where your owned, earned, and paid media work together

EARNED MEDIA

- Digital PR
- Media placements
- TV or podcast interviews
- Organic social mentions
- Organic reviews
- Reviews
- Social mentions
- Partnerships (if not paid)
- Ambassadors (if not paid)

PAID MEDIA

- Pay per click
- Display ads
- Retargeting
- Paid influencer
- Affiliate
- Social media ads
- SEO if not organic

OWNED MEDIA

- Website
- Social channels
- Blog
- LinkedIn
- Email marketing

I like to use a handy illustration to further place paid, earned, and owned media in the context of advertising, marketing, and public relations, which all eventually contribute to branding. The advertising box corresponds to paid media. It's you saying, over and over again, that you're the best startup in the whole dang world. The marketing box pertains to owned media. If you say once, directly, that you're the best startup in the whole world, it's likely part of your marketing. Now for the holy grail: the public relations box is about earned media. When someone else says your startup is the best startup in the whole world, then you've won earned media. Lastly, an entire brand is forged in the minds of your audience. Your audience takes in the paid, earned, and owned media and comes up with their own feelings about your startup.

Yes, feelings. I know some of you are pulling your hair out because you wish there were a dashboard to analyze the permutations of emotions on a minute-by-minute basis. Feelings are complex, difficult to measure, and change often, and that's because we're all selling to humans.[9] Whether you sell multimillion-dollar enterprise drone surveillance to the government or mushroom powder to a Gen Z consumer with IBS, a human is making a decision, and humans are horribly fickle. That's why a brand can be a darling one day and canceled the next. Humans determine this.

---

9   Though I can't wait for an AI to hire a PR agency to "fix" perceptions. That will be the day.

"This is a great brand."	"Trust me, they're a great brand."
MARKETING	PUBLIC RELATIONS
"This is a great brand! This is a great brand! This is a great brand!"	"I understand it's a great brand."
ADVERTISING	BRANDING

We can't do much to alter who we all sell to (those dang humans), but now you have a grasp on what paid, earned, and owned media are and how all three contribute to your venture-backed startup's brand. Often, a startup will begin with its owned media because it's fast and relatively cheap. From there, later-stage startups, post-Series A or B, will weave in earned media, choosing to spend some budget on PR agencies or freelance publicists if not relying on their venture funds' platform teams. Again, this is often cheaper than a full-blown paid media campaign. (More on hiring help in Chapter 9.) Eventually, a sizable startup may run and invest in all three areas of media. To be clear, though, it's quite unusual for a late-stage startup to *only* conduct a strong earned media campaign with no paid or owned media or to *only* run a bunch of paid media with no owned or earned media. There are rare examples, but I'd be quite a suspicious investor if I saw that you were running a Super Bowl ad and full-page inserts in the *Financial Times* but didn't have a blog or an up-to-date LinkedIn page.

COMMON REASONS FOR SEEKING EARNED MEDIA

To close out this chapter, and before we head further into your Flack Fairy understanding of messaging, what journalists want, how to reach them, and more, I'll share four common reasons why venture-backed startup founders have come to us over the years to help with their earned media. There are more reasons beyond these four, but I hope these serve as a benchmark as you consider what earned media could look like for your startup and why you should consider pursuing it.

The first reason startups seek earned media is overall perception. A Series A startup may have just twenty employees working in a warehouse off El Camino Real, but it's trying to look far bigger to all kinds of its audiences, such as potential customers, coveted talent, future investors, industry influencers, and so on. If you have twenty media placements on your website, for instance, an audience may believe your startup is "bigger" than you actually are.

Related to overall perception is sales signaling, a second reason venture-backed startups want to start securing earned media. To be clear, PR is not your outsourced sales team. However, great media placements—again, because we all sell to humans—can make an impression. Positive media coverage can also serve as a nice touchpoint, which I cover in Chapter 12 in relation to how PR can help your sales and marketing teams. Also in the "sales signaling" bucket is fundraising. Handfuls of venture-backed startups have hired us because they want to start the next round of funding conversations with potential investors. I cover this more in Chapter 12 as well, but the fact remains that venture capitalists are humans too, and they hate to miss out on the hottest startup that could be seeking capital sometime in the near future. As I say, ABR (Always Be Raising).

A third reason for bringing on PR help is to hire talent. It's common for a venture-backed startup to work with us to announce a certain round of funding so potential talent can see third-party validation that the startup appears to be doing well, at least inasmuch as it was able to raise money from notable venture capitalists. Top talent wants to work on exciting visions with compelling founders, and they also need to know a startup is on good financial ground.

Lastly, solid media placements can be part of your competitive moat. Any of your competitors can buy a bigger ad, offer better pricing, or copy the content from your blog overnight, but it's incredibly difficult for them to catch up to you if you have dozens of earned media placements in top-tier outlets. But before we get into top-tier media and what journalists at those outlets want, let's look at a fundamental component we're going to need before talking with the media: your messaging.

CHAPTER 1 SUMMARY POINTS

- PR can be a powerful vehicle to accelerate your funding and eventual exit.
- Paid, earned, and owned are the three common "buckets" of media, and PR sits in the "earned" one.
- Startups deploy PR campaigns for various reasons, but perception and digging a deep competitive moat that is hard for competitors to match are common reasons to consider investing in earned media.

Chapter 2

Landing Your Messaging

————

At this point, you may be fired up to get rolling on your earned media campaign, but before you do anything, from pitching a journalist to submitting your startup for an award, your messaging needs to be on point. This is fundamental to being a Flack Fairy, someone dangerous and dominating in PR who makes it look easy. We'll get there.

The first thing to cover in this chapter is why your messaging is so important and why it needs to be tight and consistent.

I hear some of you already: "Oh, I can explain my startup for the next two hours no problem!" The problem is that no one has two hours to try and understand what your startup is doing or why it exists, particularly the media. Solid messaging gets everyone on your team speaking the exact same words succinctly, including you. Further, it ensures that all your various outlets, from postcards at a conference booth to internal memos you send to your team, are consistent. This ultimately helps your sales prospects, potential investors, the market, and the media understand why you are distinct.

"Yeah, I get it," you say. "But we know exactly what we're building." Here's a little test. Can you tell me why, what, and how your startup does what it does in sixty seconds or less? Bonus: Can everyone who works for you say it in sixty seconds or less as well? Probably not, and that's okay. That's part of why you're reading this book, and you're like most venture-backed founders I meet. More than 70 percent of startups we work with, even the later-stage ones, have fuzzy messaging. Often, it was clear and condensed at one point, but things changed, as they so often do at startups. What we aim to do, however, is to get messaging down pat so when we knock on a reporter's digital door, we know how to convey the incredible startup you're building. Let's look at positioning versus messaging, some types of messaging, and some examples to get you thinking about your messaging.

Messaging and positioning go hand in hand. But positioning is often done internally, as a team, and fleshes out why your startup is distinct from competitors. Messaging is what goes on outside of your team, in the external world. It takes your internal positioning and conveys it to the public.

There are various forms of messaging, such as product and persona messaging, but the one we like to focus on initially as publicists is brand messaging. Like a pitch deck, there's not an "absolute" or one way a brand messaging framework has to be. I'm including a handy diagram to show the components of a brand messaging framework, but I want to point out it's short. It's not eleven typed, single-spaced pages. Ideally, you can print out your brand messaging framework on *one* page and glance at it while being interviewed by a journalist if you're doing a phone call. A framework is not meant to be the novel about your startup's entire past and its future, though so many founders get tripped up on how condensed this one page can be. Don't fret. I'm going to give several examples for each component of a brand messaging framework so you'll have plenty to get your ideas brewing. In addition, this overview is just meant to be that: a quick sketch that gives you enough to be dangerous and dominating as a Flack Fairy. Then, you can determine a plan and how to do a deep dive on your messaging, which you can conduct internally with someone who has a great grasp on messaging or with the help of external pros, which I cover in Chapter 9.

VISION

The vision of your startup is usually at the top of a branding messaging document. It's the incredible thing you see for the world if your startup is successful. Airbnb's is, "Belong anywhere."[10] Amazon's is a bit meatier: "Our vision is to be earth's most customer centric company; to build a place where people can come to find and discover anything they might want to buy online."[11]

MISSION

Next is your mission, which is what you're going to do to make that vision actually happen. Instagram's mission, for instance, is to, "Capture and share the world's moments."[12] NVIDIA's mission is to, "Develop high-performance computers that scientists, researchers, artists, and creators from around the world use to create the future and improve lives."[13]

---

10 Daniel Pereira, "Airbnb Mission and Vision Statement," The Business Model Analyst, June 10, 2023, https://businessmodelanalyst.com/airbnb-mission-and-vision-statement/.

11 Patrick Hull, "Be Visionary. Think Big.," *Forbes*, December 19, 2012, https://www.forbes.com/sites/patrickhull/2012/12/19/be-visionary-think-big/.

12 "Instagram: Everything You Need to Know," *Social Stamina* (blog), March 21, 2022, https://www.socialstamina.com/blog/everything-you-need-to-know-about-instagram.

13 "Corporate Social Responsibility (CSR) Directive," NVIDIA, August 26, 2020, https://www.nvidia.cn/content/dam/en-zz/Solutions/about-us/documents/nvidia-corporate-responsibility-directive.pdf.

BRAND PROMISE

You might then have a brand promise or a value proposition conveying what you guarantee to a customer. It's like a pledge as you accomplish your mission. My favorite is Geico's, which is, "Fifteen minutes could save you 15 percent or more on car insurance."[14]

TARGET AUDIENCES

There are usually a few, up to perhaps five, audiences you're aiming your messaging toward, and your target certainly shouldn't be "the world." Plaid, for instance, targets financial partners in the automotive, banking, financial services, crypto, real estate, and healthcare sectors.[15] Audiences may also include your employees, investors, and regulatory groups.

TAGLINE

A tagline is a catchy, quick, and ideally unforgettable phrase, like Apple's "Think Different" or Google's former "Don't be evil" motto.[16] A tagline is like the written version of your brand. As soon as you say it, people should say, "Oh, that's X."

---

14 Amanda Aronczyk, Erika Beras, Mary Childs, Nick Fountain, Sarah Gonzalez, Jeff Guo, Alexi Horowitz-Ghazi, and Kenny Malone, hosts, *Planet Money*, podcast, "The Gecko Effect," produced by Alex Goldmark, NPR, June 10, 2022, https://www.npr.org/2022/06/01/1102496094/the-gecko-effect.

15 "You'll Be in Good Company," Plaid, accessed December 1, 2024, https://plaid.com/customer-stories/library/.

16 Rob Siltanen, "The Real Story Behind Apple's 'Think Different' Campaign," *Forbes*, December 10, 2021, https://www.forbes.com/sites/onmarketing/2011/12/14/the-real-story-behind-apples-think-different-campaign/; Shirin Ghaffary and Alex Kantrowitz, "'Don't Be Evil' Isn't a Normal Company Value. But Google Isn't a Normal Company," *Vox*, February 16, 2021, https://www.vox.com/recode/2021/2/16/22280502/google-dont-be-evil-land-of-the-giants-podcast.

TONE OF VOICE

This is how your brand sounds. Cybersecurity startups, such as CrowdStrike, are often steely and strong, whereas creative companies, like Canva, are more lighthearted. Canva's tone of voice is "inspiring," "empowering," and "human."[17]

SUPPORTING PROOF/DIFFERENTIATORS

This area is reserved for the numbers, data points, and explicit reasons why your startup stands apart from others. A lot of founders get mixed up here as they want to say there are eighteen reasons why they stand apart from competitors. This area of your brand messaging framework should answer a reporter when they ask, "So what makes you so different from X and Y competitors?"

I've included the first draft of a brand messaging framework I put together for my fund BIG (Bad Ideas Group) to further illustrate what messaging looks like. As I said, just like a pitch deck, there's no "absolute" or "right" way to do a branding messaging document. The important thing is to get everyone on your team literally on the same page and consistently saying everything on that page.

One note of caution: One page seems alluringly easy. "We'll hammer this out in one hour, no problem," you're thinking. There's a reason Blaise Pascal wrote, "The present letter is a very long one, simply because I had no leisure to make it shorter."[18] Like a twelve-slide pitch deck, a one-page branding messaging document can take some time and pain.

Here's the bottom line: Messaging absolutely matters, and

---

17 "Tone of Voice," Canva Brand, accessed December 23, 2024, https://public.canva.site/tone-of-voice.

18 Blaise Pascal, *The Provincial Letters*, trans. Thomas M'Crie, ed. O. W. Wight (Hurd and Houghton, 1866), 417.

before you talk with anyone in the media, you need to ensure it is crisp and sharp. Think of it as an ironed white shirt, not a bulky puffer vest or a crumpled sweatshirt. If you feel compelled to put this book down to get cranking on your messaging for a while, great. I'll be here. When you're ready, in the next few chapters, we're going to get into what the media want, who they are, and what kind of pitches tend to resonate with them.

Brand messaging framework			
Vision	[Aspirational picture of the world in this future]		
Mission	[How you are going to help make your vision a reality]		
Overall value proposition	[Overall value-creating proposition of your company]		
Target audience	[Your ideal customer]		
Tagline	[Catchphrase or slogan you use to describe your company or product]		
Tone of voice	[The personality traits of your brand and voice you want to embody]		
Brand pillars	[Theme that sets your brand apart]	[Theme that sets your brand apart]	[Theme that sets your brand apart]
Proof points	[Details and differentiators that support the brand pillar]	[Details and differentiators that support the brand pillar]	[Details and differentiators that support the brand pillar]

BIG VENTURES

Mission	Our mission is for people and the planet to live better and last longer by investing in Series A-stage startups in the health and climate tech space.
Values	Total transparency. Radical candor. Better together.
Target Audience(s)	Primary for 2025: LPs who invest in progressive funds making bets on technology that positively impacts people and the planet
Tone of Voice	"Costco casual": We sell the best in the world, but you push your own cart. It's a club, and we check the receipts.
Summary Message	BIG Ventures is the VC fund for bad ideas, good stories, and great outcomes. We grow unicorns, spur IPOs, and make exits happen for our climate tech and health tech startups by deploying the undeniable power of media relations alongside capital at the Series A-level and beyond. We believe stories move the world, and money measures it.

Differentiators	Supporting Examples
LP and exited women GPs alongside team that's been together for ten-plus years	The general partners of BIG, two women, come from decades of startup experience as well as a PR team that's been together for a decade: • Dr. Beck Bamberger: PR tech CEO, exited BAM in 2023 to a public global group with a team of thirty-plus • Regina Bernal: Head of a family office with a global network of founders and VCs. Specialized in guiding tech and life science entrepreneurs to secure millions in startup capital, with successful exits. Launched SoCal's fastest-growing diverse talent leadership program, partnering with forty-plus companies across the innovation sector. TEDx speaker • BAM, the agency that was sold to an international agency in 2023, has an average tenure of seven years, an unheard-of longevity in the PR/agency space, and with nearly a 4.8-star rating on Glassdoor.
PR machine that's spurred twenty-plus exits and unicorns	BIG's PR army, a team that has worked together for ten-plus years at BAM, ensures each investment gets a full PR and marketing team from check to exit. BIG's PR army helped the exits and unicorns of: • Flock Freight • Pacaso • Unite Us • Getaround • Culture Amp • Back Market • Udacity • DispatchHealth • Pivot Bio • Arcadia • RoadRunner • Xeneta • Upstart • Credit Sesame • Adore Me • SOPHIA GENETICS • Veyo
Unbeatable deal flow from forty-plus annual events plus comms community of 491 VC funds	Over ten-plus years, BAM's forty-plus annual gatherings have cemented its reputation among VCs, founders, and top-tier media. BIG continues the curation of high-value gatherings that spark deep relationships, media coverage, and investments such as with: • VC Comms Con: the annual gathering of 120-plus VC comms professionals worldwide • Minds in Montana: the annual ranch gathering for BIG's LPs • Media Matchmaking Day: quarterly speed dating events attended by forty-plus founders and forty-plus top-tier media • BIG's Progressive Dinner Parties: intimate dinner affairs around the globe

CHAPTER 2 SUMMARY POINTS

- If you can't explain the why, how, and what of your startup in under a minute, you need to get this nailed down before launching a PR campaign or talking with anyone in media.
- There are all kinds of messaging, and there isn't "one" way to do it. Publicists often look at "brand messaging," which includes the vision, mission, persona, taglines, and distinctions.
- Brand messaging usually fits on one page. It is terse and tight on purpose.

Chapter 3

Understanding What Journalists Want

Alright, Flack Fairy. At this point, you understand earned, paid, and owned media; why you may want to leverage earned media; and how critical tight messaging is. Now, we're getting to a topic every founder seems to be obsessed with: what journalists want. I know some of you flipped right to this chapter, and that's okay, of course.

Journalists, much like VCs, seem immensely powerful and evasive. Understanding exactly how a VC issues a check for millions of dollars to a startup is just as daunting as understanding how a reporter writes up a story about a startup and publishes it. In this chapter, I'll spell out what journalists want, based on fifteen-plus years of working with them, along with my insights from interviewing hundreds of them one by one on the podcast I host for OnePitch, *Coffee with a Journalist*.[19] I have some juicy data too.

---

19   OnePitch is an SaaS startup I founded to help publicists pitch media more accurately. It's a classic startup story: I experienced a big problem firsthand and knew a far better solution could exist. For years, I've interviewed journalists on a weekly basis for our podcast. Search *Coffee with a Journalist* wherever you get your podcasts if you want to do a deep dive on a particular media person.

Let's first understand the insane job of a journalist. You have an insane job as a founder, yes, but you don't pump out written copy or content, such as TV segments about unfolding developments in the world, from scratch on an hourly basis. It's a lot. In addition, journalists are on deadlines dictated by the pace of the world. Some stories need to be filed within hours or even minutes of their assignment.[20]

When I was just starting out in TV newsrooms years ago, my mind was blown. I could not believe that six hours of television was created *every* day—and to be clear, every day of the *year*. Today, I read the daily print editions of *The Wall Street Journal*, *The New York Times*, and *Financial Times* and am gobsmacked at how many pages of content are produced *every* day. Think about that for a moment. Could your startup crank out a product of such quality *every* day? I am humbled by newsrooms, and I hope you are too.

Now that we've established that journalists are doing remarkably hard jobs, let's get into what they want. Based on the interviews I've conducted for the *Coffee with a Journalist* podcast and the thousands of stories that we at BAM have placed for venture-backed startups, here are some main takeaways and data:

- No niceties: The media don't want a paragraph in a pitch about how much you *loved* their last story or how great you hope their day is going. For some founders, this seems counterintuitive, but for the vast majority of journalists, a shockingly succinct pitch is the way to go.
- No obscurity: Being vague or coy is a big pet peeve for journalists. Spell out whom and what your pitch is about rather than alluding to a "big investor" or "important partner" who will be working with your startup.

---

20 An exception is long-form investigative stories, which may take months or even more than a year to craft.

- No fluff: A pitch you send to a journalist shouldn't claim "explosive growth" or "revolutionary traction in X industry."
- No "spray and pray": The "spray and pray" approach, where pitches are sent out en masse with little targeting, often yields nothing. It's similar to sending out an email to seven hundred VCs and just changing the opening greeting to the person's first name, à la, "Hi Bob—I'd love to tell you about my startup that is currently raising..." Journalists, like VCs, can spot a spam pitch in a second.
- No delays: What happens if you send a pitch, get a response from a journalist, and then don't respond immediately? Stories are killed because publicists or startups aren't quick enough.
- No back and forths: Make a journalist's job as easy as possible. Don't exchange twenty emails to set up an interview when you could simply list your availability with several options in the first response.
- No socials or text: Journalists don't want to be pitched on other platforms like Instagram or TikTok. The same goes for texting, if you somehow managed to get a reporter's cell phone number. The email inbox is still the preferred vehicle, as we'll see in the following stats.

THE JOURNALIST'S INBOX

Let's get into some data direct from journalists who have been on *Coffee with a Journalist* with me and come from outlets including Bloomberg, *The New York Times, Axios, Time,* The Information, *TechCrunch,* CNBC, *Fast Company, Bustle, Vogue, Travel & Leisure,* Parents.com, *Elle, Forbes, The Wall Street Journal, USA Today, Financial Times, Mashable, Business Insider, Wired, The Washington Post,* NPR, *Politico,* and more. I present these stats so you have some raw info about what journalists prefer, though preferences do vary, of course. The range of journalists is wide here, meaning these stats don't just pertain to tech reporters who cover venture-backed startups but rather encompass hundreds of journalists' feedback, a decent sample size. My OnePitch team crunched the numbers from the verbal answers on the podcast, and here's what shook out:

- Ninety-six percent of journalists want to be pitched in their inboxes, not via social media, text, or other means.
- Sixty-four percent of journalists receive at least two hundred pitches a week. Only 14 percent receive less than fifty pitches a week.
- Ninety percent of journalists use pitches from publicists, founders, and companies to help create their stories.
- Ninety-three percent of journalists say the subject line of a pitch is at least "mildly" or "very important" when it comes to determining whether the pitch is opened or not.
- More than 90 percent of journalists do not have an "inbox zero" discipline. Some journalists have more than fifty thousand unread emails, most of which are pitches that simply go unread because of poor subject lines.
- More than half of the journalists say they are not actively speaking with sources, but 42 percent say they create many of their stories through talking with important sources within their beats.
- Only 50 percent of journalists are open to getting on a call, while others feel they don't have the bandwidth to chat with a source, publicist, or startup just to check in or see what could be a viable story down the road.

Further, to better illuminate some of the stats above, here is what journalists have said on *Coffee with a Journalist*:

"If the subject line is something related to my beat, I would open it and see what's in that. Sometimes, it's just clearly irrelevant, so I just skip those."

—REPORTER FROM *THE OBSERVER*

"The more detail, the better. Especially if it has 'entrepreneur' in that subject line or 'small business owner,' I'm definitely going to click on it."

—REPORTER FROM *BUSINESS INSIDER*

"I tend to look for the subject line, which may catch my interest. That said, I'm not a fan of somebody writing "TIME SENSITIVE" in all caps, although I do understand that that is often a thing."

—REPORTER FROM *FAST COMPANY*

"I think [calls are] one of the most important things that I can do to facilitate relationships, as well as learn more about companies within my industries that I cover."

—REPORTER FROM CRUNCHBASE

"Often, a pitch for a coffee with someone in the old days, or now it'd be a Zoom call these days, and to get to know someone else in the field, someone who may have something to say that's interesting about a topic that I'm reporting on...I'm very happy to make time for those sorts of things."

—REPORTER FROM *THE WALL STREET JOURNAL*

"Just send me the idea. The shorter, the better. I just get a lot of pitches that are like one thousand words long, and I can't even look at those."

—REPORTER FROM PROTOCOL

"If it's like a deadline-sensitive thing or if it's an embargo...make that clear, and then to spell my name right."

—REPORTER FROM CNN

"I really need a news peg. I really need to know why I'm getting this story now...tell me what's new or different, and give it some business context."

—REPORTER FROM CNBC

In short, journalists want pitches in their email inboxes that don't waste time. Being direct, immediately available, and specific so journalists know your pitch and subject line are just for them is the jam. Reporters are squeezed for their time and attention. I know you may feel a bit deflated reading the above stats and quotes. How are you going to compete with all those other pitches in a journalist's email inbox, let alone get your pitch opened? Moreover, how do you even get journalists to know about you if they've never heard of you? That's what our next chapter is for, Flack Fairy.

CHAPTER 3 SUMMARY POINTS

- A journalist's email inbox is where you want to send a pitch.
- Journalists' email inboxes are flooded, so to get your email opened, be direct and succinct in the subject line.
- Journalists don't care who sends them pitches. If a pitch is good and timely, then they can use it. Ultimately, don't waste a journalist's time.

Chapter 4

Pitches That Placed

———

This is a meaty chapter on purpose. I want to convey how varied and far sweeping the pitches that nab the media's attention can be. The truth is that there is no formula for getting a pitch read by a journalist, much like there isn't a prescription for raising $30 million from a VC. Pitching, whether to the media or to VCs, is an art. Like pitching to VCs, anyone can do it. You don't need a badge or credentials to email a journalist, and most journalists don't mind hearing from founders directly, as mentioned in the last chapter. That said, the reason you hire a publicist or PR agency, which we'll get to in Chapter 9, is for their efficiency in having existing relationships with journalists and knowing how to not waste time.

MAKING MEDIA MOMENTS

Let's look first at what's *not* a story to pitch. I like to burst some bubbles right up front because we do spend a lot of time, it seems, explaining how some of these moments are just not (typically) of interest to journalists despite a founder's insistence. You're going to know better because you're a Flack Fairy. That said, we like a "yes, and" approach, and there are some ways to expand on the following "moments" to garner media interest, which will be discussed later in this chapter. Here we go.

YOU'VE DEVELOPED A NEW FEATURE

You've just launched a new feature to your platform, which is still offered at the same price and to the same audience. While your team might have worked on it for months, realize that to the outside world, it's not a big development. *What could work*: Consider pitching this to trade-specific media. Those outlets typically test features and review them for niche audiences, which might be ideal for your specific industry, such as in supply-chain or human-resources applications.

YOU'VE LANDED A MAJOR CLIENT
WHO CAN'T BE NAMED AT ALL

You finally landed the whale, but the whale doesn't want to be seen in association with your company just yet. This is common for enterprise startups, which often have the "promotion" terms of their agreements redlined. If you're not able to share the client's name, you can try to classify the win with something along the lines of, "A major player in the home-refinance market." But heads up: Media outlets tend to be turned off by the lack of transparency of not naming names. *What could work*: Look for new partners who are thrilled at the results you've delivered and are more than happy to tout your partnership. Then, you'll have data and insights that you can point to.

YOU SPOKE ON A PANEL

You're excited to be on a panel and at the center of a stage overlooking a big audience. But unless you lead a huge startup, a quote that you dropped during the discussion likely isn't of major interest to the media. *What could work*: Recycle that panel conversation into a thought-leadership piece that you can leverage on your owned platforms, such as LinkedIn, Medium, your blog, and Instagram stories. I cover this more in Chapter 12.

YOU WON AN AWARD

Did your startup make it onto a list of fastest-growing companies along with hundreds of other companies? Or was your business named one of the best places to work along with ninety-nine other brands? As great as these recognitions are, they don't necessarily warrant further praise by the media. *What could work*: Wrap the distinctions into your press kit, pitches, career pages, and owned media platforms, including your newsletters, investor-relations decks, and careers page. Instead of the standard blog post saying, "We're so honored with this award..." consider digging deeper with your C-suite into why this award matters now, why you got this award, and what you're doing next because of this recognition.

YOU HAVE A NEW C-SUITE HIRE

A C-suite hire isn't usually going to turn heads in the media unless you really landed an industry all-star. There's an enormous volume of companies out there scoring top-notch talent every day. *What could work*: Tie the new-hire announcement into a funding or other major milestone, and pitch that entire story. You certainly can announce the new hire on your owned media platforms. If the new hire is well known in your industry, trade media might cover the move.

YOU ADDED AN ADVISOR OR BOARD MEMBER

If a major celebrity in your industry has joined your board, then you may have hot news to share. Otherwise, having a new advisor or board member isn't too enticing to the media. *What could work*: See if this new advisor or board member is willing to be featured in future press opportunities. If so, be sure to give them the proper media training so you're ready when that opportunity comes knocking.

YOUR COMPANY IS NOT DYING (AND OTHER TRICKS OF PERCENTAGES AND "GROWTH")

The fact that your startup boasts 1,056 percent year-over-year growth is definitely great news for you, but it's not newsworthy at face value. *What could work*: Share hard data on your year-over-year revenue and customer growth along with insights into the industry trends driving your startup's success.

Now that you know what typically isn't a story, let's get to the good stuff about stories that are of interest to the media. I'm sharing several "pitches that placed" in a variety of categories we see often for startups. Note that I've stripped out pertinent and sensitive details from these pitches. This list also isn't exhaustive but is meant to arm you with enough clear examples of pitches to ensure you're sharper than your PR team and a true Flack Fairy. A theme you'll notice in a number of these pitches is what I call "plating the story." Journalists are tight on time, as we discussed. When you can provide a journalist with enough aspects of a full, delicious story, they're more likely to want to eat it. Let's see how this concept plays out in several of the following pitch examples.

FUNDING

Yes, funding announcements are still viable media stories to a handful of tech media outlets. Here's one example that landed in *TechCrunch*:

Subject Line: Industrial Al Software Secures Funding to Deploy New Sustainability Features

Hi XX,

(Startup) will be announcing a growth financing round that will enable the company to deploy new Al sustainability features for the steel, cement, and chemical sectors on Wednesday, June 21. With this news right up your alley, I wanted to give you first dibs at it.

As you know, the industrial sector is notoriously hard to decarbonize, and hardware solutions like carbon capture and storage come with hefty price tags and daunting implementation processes. That's why investors are doubling down on solutions like (Startup)'s white-box (explainable) Al software that requires no capital expenditure and little Al expertise by engineers and makes an immediate positive impact on efficiency, Scope 3 emissions, and profits.

(Startup)'s customers include $10B+ industrials, including Gerdau, Covestro, CELSA Nordic, and more. The company has uncovered upward of $XM in savings and reduced more than one hundred thousand tons of carbon emissions for its customers to date.

Can I share more details with you under embargo? I can also connect you with (founder), co-founder and CEO, and the lead investor, if interested in pursuing.

Please let me know at your earliest.

Notice that this pitch includes a date right in the first sentence, as well as numbers and customer names along with who is available to speak. This is a good "plate," which a journalist took.

Here's another funding example that got picked up by *Business Insider*:

Subject Line: (Startup) Secures $20M Series D Extension

Hi XX,

On November 15, (Startup), a leader in comprehensive sustainable waste management, will announce the close of $20 million in a Series D extension round led by (VC fund), the largest venture capital firm focused on technology for the global real estate industry. This totals $90 million in funding in just ten months for (Startup).

The quick and dirty of it:

- During a market that has proved difficult for growth, (Startup) has secured another $20 million following a $70 million Series D in January and the acquisition of (another startup) in October.
- The funds will support continued growth of (Startup)'s core business and technology.
- (VC fund) led this round following the close of its $500 million (name of its fund), the largest private fund formed to decarbonize the real estate industry.
- (Startup) will support sustainable waste-management streams for some of the world's most prominent commercial real estate owners and operators.

Can I share the full details with you under embargo? I can also connect you with (VC), co-founder and Managing Partner of (VC fund), and (founder's name), founder and CEO of (Startup).

Once again, the available people are named and listed, and this pitch uses the prominence of its VC fund to add more to the story.

EXPERT SOURCES

The media certainly need reliable, quick, and qualified folks to speak with. Here are two "pitches that placed." The first landed in Bloomberg.

Subject Line: Connect with (name of founder), Serial Entrepreneur, on AI, ChatGPT, and the Future of Work and Humanity?

Hi XX,

As society fears the repercussions of ChatGPT and other trending AI models, (name of founder), serial entrepreneur and current chairman and co-founder of (Startup), argues that AI will not replace us—it is going to free humanity of repetitive, boring work; open new doors professionally; and unleash our ultimate creativity. AI is going to play a huge role in driving human progress and growing our economies.

Following (name of founder)'s presence and panel on this very topic at the 2023 World Government Summit held just last month, are you interested in learning more about (name of founder)'s perspective?

If so, I'd be happy to find a time to connect the two of you to discuss how AI is going to play a positive role in building economies and propelling humanity forward.

Let me know!

This pitch names a pretty prominent founder in the subject line and leverages his panel's talking points to court the media's attention.

Here's a pitch that outlines the source's quotes in the pitch itself, which helped this founder's comments land in *The Wall Street Journal*:

Subject Line: [Source] VCs Cash Out via Secondaries as IPO and M&A Activity Fall Behind

Hi XX,

Moves like raising the largest fund ever dedicated to investing in venture secondaries is saying a lot about how VCs are looking to navigate the current market.

If you are pondering any stories about the alternative options LPs are weighing as they look to cash out, I'd like to put you in touch with (name of VC), Managing Director at (venture fund), a SF-based $750M VC fund by (billionaire LP).

(Name of VC) would be happy to share more on his POV:

- The state of secondaries as it relates to startups and funds: "(Quote)."
- The evolution of secondaries, how they are approached, and why they are much less taboo today: "(Quote)."
- How the opening of the IPO market could boost the interest of buyers in the secondary market: "(Quote)."

Let me know if there is a date and time that works best for the two of you to chat further!

CUSTOMERS

Customers, particularly the big names that are publicly traded, are excellent to leverage in pitches. However, you must have explicit permission to pitch such stories. Often, we work in tandem with the PR team of a big brand to ensure everything is aboveboard. Here are two more "pitches that placed," the first on CNBC as a trend story and the other in a trade publication:

Subject Line: [Embargo] (Institute) Reports Increased Recovery of 1,400 Cans per Day with Robots

Hi XX,

In September, the (institute) funded a (Startup) robot at (facility), an MRF in (state) to save more than 1M aluminum beverage cans annually from the landfill. Two months later, (institute) and (facility) are excited to report (Startup) is seeing up to 1,400 used beverage cans (UBCs) per day, with its robot recovering a vast majority to enable a circular supply chain.

(Institute)'s research highlighted that up to one in four aluminum beverage cans was missorted at a typical MRF, resulting in substantial revenue loss. They chose (Startup)'s robotic solution to help resolve this problem given their capabilities, including:

- Enabling deployment within a few hours with no downtime or retrofits.
- Tracking of robotic performance, with 24/7 professional monitoring and minute-by-minute data on what types of materials are coming across lines.
- The robot is on track to capture approximately thirty-two thousand pounds of UBCs annually, equivalent to over one million UBCs per

year. This will help expedite aluminum production in a sustainable way since 93 percent of recycled aluminum beverage cans are used to make new cans and require 94 percent less energy compared to the traditional aluminum process.

The embargo will lift on (date). Can I share the full case study with you and connect you with executives from (Startup), (institute), or (facility) to further discuss the results beforehand?

This pitch is tight with its numbers and leverages not only a national institute but a major facility. Notice the subject line indicates an embargo piece of news, a creditable institute the reporter knows (given our experience with the reporter), a specific number (1,400), and how (a robot) they got a result.

Let's look at this other example that drops the name of Amazon, not as a partner but as a competitor. This is a bolder strategy as calling out the dragon you're trying to slay certainly makes the dragon's nostrils flare, but such an approach can be effective in securing media coverage if you're willing to take the risk.

Subject Line: DTC Brand (name of brand) Invests in Warehouse Robotics System to Compete with Amazon

Hi XX,

Today, (name of brand), an LA-based (description of brand) company, completed the installation of its brand-new warehouse robotics system by (Startup).

(Name of brand) is the first US e-commerce brand to use this automated warehouse system to fulfill orders and complete same-day delivery to keep up with and outperform big-box retailers and giants like Amazon. (Startup)'s warehouse robotics system was created by AutoStore, the world's leading warehouse-automation company, to address two major challenges e-commerce brands face: high labor costs and high customer expectations regarding order fulfillment and delivery.

Overcoming these challenges isn't possible without automation, which is why (name of brand) decided to go all-in and is now capable of picking and packing 360 orders per hour, reducing labor costs by up to 80 percent, and saving hundreds of thousands of dollars annually.

I wanted to share this news with you in case it's of interest. I've included a copy of the press release with more information below, and here is a video of the warehouse robotics system. It's basically the hardware version of Shopify for e-commerce businesses; pretty cool. I'd be happy to schedule a virtual demo of (name of brand)'s (corporate name) system and/or an interview with (Startup)'s CEO, (name), or (name of brand's) Head of Commerce, (name). Just let me know!

This pitch used a well-known brand name, clear metrics, and a "dragon" to spell out the story. I love customer stories, so here's another pitch that placed, which earned a story in *Time* because of a major partnership:

Subject Line: [Embargo] On Heels of New OSHA Heat Rule, (Startup) Will Protect (big-name company) Workers Globally

Hi XX,

Last week, OSHA proposed a rule that would require employers to develop an injury and illness prevention plan to control heat hazards in workplaces. If finalized, the rule would help protect ~36M workers in indoor and outdoor settings. As lawmakers play catch up to meet today's worker-protection needs, (Startup) has already been filling the gaps to protect workers at (impressive number)+ Fortune 500 companies.

Next week, the company will announce a three-year MSA with (big-name company) to equip its industrial frontline workers with (Startup's technology portal). See below for the details:

- **WHO:** (Startup), a (description of startup). (Name of product) is a wearable (description) solution that measures sweat loss, sodium loss, skin temperature, and movement to provide actionable rehydration strategies in real time to industrial workers ahead of adverse dehydration events.
- **WHAT:** The (big-name company) and (Startup) have agreed to deploy (product name) across (big-name company)'s industrial frontline workers, beginning in the US this summer with plans to expand to global markets.
- **WHY:** Climate change continues to intensify across the globe. Cumulative exposure to extreme heat is proven to cause cognitive decline and physiological dysfunction and impede the physical performance required for industrial occupations. This collaboration empowers (big-name company) to provide its frontline workforce with the latest safety technology to ensure their health and well-being.
- **WHEN:** (Date details of embargo).

Can I share the press release with you under embargo? I can also connect you with (founder of Startup) and (name), VP of Innovation and President of Technology Ventures for (big-name company), to discuss the news and why employers should take a proactive approach to protect workers.

REPORTS AND DATA

Data that you specifically and exclusively own or an enticing report that showcases findings in your industry can also land media coverage. Before I show a few examples, let's cover what "data" of media interest actually means. I called it the "DATA approach."

D: DISTINCT

Can you absolutely assure others that your data is distinct to *your* startup? Or does the data you tout come from a third party, such as an API, government agency, or consulting group like Deloitte? Distinct data is the most important aspect the media will consider. If it's not your data and yours alone, it's unlikely to be interesting to journalists. One of our notable clients in the HR space claimed they had a new report that would be ideal for top-tier media. The report, unfortunately, was nothing more than a repackaging of an annual report from a major industry association. In short, we couldn't use it for any media stories.

A: AUDIENCE

The second aspect of data we consider is the potential audience. Is your data worthy of an audience? It's a subjective question, but a few examples should help clarify what I mean. Every journalist reports for a media outlet with a defined audience. The larger your data's audience, the more likely a larger media outlet will be interested in it. For example, one of our proptech security startups tracked data on which types of buildings were being accessed during the first months of the COVID-19 pandemic. Its data identified that churches and cannabis shops were often visited throughout the early days of quarantine. Thanks to that data, we had a solid story that showed that for grass and God, people didn't seem to be deterred by stay-at-home mandates. Using that data, we secured a lineup of top-tier media opportunities.

As a counterexample, consider the time Uber allegedly flaunted how it tracks celebrities' whereabouts.[21] To be certain, this was data only Uber had, but the audience for this sensitive data should have stayed within Uber and was therefore not worthy of any exposure. The privacy of your data needs to be considered.

T: TIME-BOUND

Time-bound is the third component to assessing the viability of a startup's data. Many founders get stuck on this item because all data is measured from one point in time to another. True, but some data takes far too long to measure and collect to be viable for press interest. For instance, an edtech startup may claim its baby app helps foster cognitive skills in adulthood, or a climate-tech startup may announce it can help reduce forest fires across the country and regrow entire forests. In both cases, it will take years for the merits of either startup to show results and be of any use to journalists.

As an extreme example, consider the happiness study conducted by Harvard University that just reported its results after starting eighty-plus years ago. No startup wants to be around for eighty years, of course. Work with your PR team to identify relevance on an annual or even quarterly basis. Many of our startups establish yearly reports, which can become consistent news moments journalists ultimately rely on.

---

21   Chris Smith, "Uber Allegedly Spied on Celebrities Like Beyoncé for Years," *New York Post*, December 13, 2016, https://nypost.com/2016/12/13/uber-allegedly-spied-on-celebrities-like-beyonce-for-years/.

A: ATTAINABLE

Finally, how attainable your data is will determine whether your PR team can present it to journalists. Often, in later-stage venture-backed startups, the data teams are large and occupied with deadlines. They don't want to hear from the PR team for data requests that may or may not be useful to a potential story. In younger startups, founders can help establish the importance of leveraging data for media relations, so routine requests become standard and not cumbersome or annoying. Further, we'll often get a set of data that looks like a pile of code spaghetti to the untrained eye of a non-data-scientist. Only large publications with strong data teams, like *The New York Times* or *The Wall Street Journal*, will be able to decipher that code. Make sure your data team can package data for the media audience so they can tell a story with the numbers.

The mathematician Clive Humby once said, "Data is the new oil. Like oil, data is valuable, but if unrefined it cannot really be used."[22] This couldn't be more true for startups as you consider how your data could be of interest to media outlets. Follow the DATA approach to assess the feasibility of your data and you'll have a decent shot at obtaining earned media coverage. Let's look now at two examples:

Subject Line: New Report + Data Find Where AI Can Play a Major Role in Combating Climate Change

Hi XX,

This past week, (founder), co-founder and chief scientist at (Startup),

---

22 Nisha Talagala, "Data As the New Oil Is Not Enough: Four Principles for Avoiding Data Fires," *Forbes*, last updated March 4, 2022, https://www.forbes.com/sites/nishatalagala/2022/03/02/data-as-the-new-oil-is-not-enough-four-principles-for-avoiding-data-fires/.

presented a draft of ICEF's latest report: (Year) Roadmap on Artificial Intelligence for Climate Change Mitigation.

The extensive research identifies the ways in which AI has the potential to make significant contributions to climate change, including greenhouse-gas-emissions monitoring; decarbonization of the power sector; discovery of novel materials; and reducing emissions from manufacturing, the food system, and road transport.

The report highlights real-time data and recent use cases to validate AI's impact so far. Pages 123–127 summarize the key findings nicely.

Later this month, (founder) will be presenting these findings at (major conference) for an important discussion on AI's potential contribution to saving our planet. Ahead of this notable event and as we close out a year hyper-focused on this issue, can I connect you with (founder) for a deep dive?

Let me know what dates and times work best.

This pitch, which landed coverage in the *Financial Times*, used two major areas of media coverage that are hot right now as of the publishing of this book: AI and climate change. Further, this pitch flexed how the founder was already presenting the report's findings at a big conference on a certain date, a stellar way to demonstrate the report's credibility as well as its timeliness. Here's another:

Subject Line: Exclusive—New Study Reveals 8+ Million Tons of Recyclables Are Going to Landfill Annually

Hi XX,

On (date), AI and robotics company (Startup) will be publishing its first-ever study revealing the shocking amount of top recyclables still ending up in landfills in the United States. The study found that:

- Collectively, (big number) million tons ($4 billion worth) of the top recyclable materials are being sent to landfills annually through losses in residential recycling and at material recycling facilities (MRFs).
- With X percent (big number; $1.7 billion worth) of these recyclables successfully diverted to recycling facilities annually, 27 percent still ends up in the landfill due to inefficiencies inside recycling facilities.
- Valuable plastics like PET make up XK tons ($211 million), HDPE make up XK tons ($98 million), PP make up XK tons ($19 million), and aluminum cans make up XK tons ($57 million) of the 27 percent landfilled by MRFs.

Today, a typical recycling facility loses up to $(big number) of recyclables annually for every ton per day they process. So, if it processes five hundred tons per day, it can lose $1 million annually. This is material that can be easily recovered with technology and made into new material, significantly contributing to a circular economy and positively impacting MRFs economically.

This study was conducted over two years by anonymous sampling in mid–large single-stream recycling facilities nationwide and on specific material types that are valuable recyclable commodities, including HDPE, aluminum, PP, and PET. It does not include glass, tin, film, and other recyclables. (Startup) used its depth-sensing cameras paired with its AI models to identify recyclables in the recycling stream as they travelled from collection operations through an MRF. The data produced was used to determine the type, volume, and value of recyclable materials being sent to landfills.

(Name), CEO and founder of (Startup), is urging recyclers globally to prioritize innovation to capture the millions of materials being lost to landfills. Yes, recycling legislation will play a crucial role in increasing the nation's recycling rate, but recycling facilities need to fix their inefficiencies to increase success and benefit the environment and economy.

Can I share the full study with you exclusively and connect you with (founder) ahead of (date)?

This pitch resulted in coverage in a notable trade publication and was detailed because of the nature of the media outlet. Note the details of dollar savings, number of tons, specific materials, and the timeframe in which the study was conducted.

TRENDS

Unlike data and reports, which often take several months, if not years, to obtain, a trend may appear seemingly overnight (but is not usually as hot as a newsjacking moment, which I will cover in the next section). If you see one emerging, then leverage your spokespersons, who can speak about it as another way to land some media coverage. Here's an example, which secured quotes in *The New York Times*:

Subject Line: Intro for (name of journalist)—(founder) at (Startup)

I saw you write Q&As with women in finance, so I wanted to offer an intro to (name of person), Head of (fancy title) at (Startup). She can discuss the ins and outs of alternative asset investing and how she is growing the alternative investment category at (Startup). She can touch on:

- How advisors can get started researching alternatives
- Common objections with alternatives and how to overcome them

With an unstable market environment, interest-rate volatility domestically, and heading into a major election year, a meaningful allocation to alternative investments can help a portfolio weather public-market uncertainty.

What do you think? Happy to get a call scheduled with (name of person).

It's a pretty pointed pitch that calls out the journalist's name in the subject line (something we do occasionally so the reporter knows the pitch is just for them) as well as why the person we teed up is of value to the reporter using current market shifts. Here's another example that got commentary placed in a *USA Today* article:

Subject Line: Intro for (name of reporter)—Millennials Are Looking for the Next Level of Investing

Hi XX,

Thanks to a booming stock market, millennials' wealth is growing at a steady pace, but many are ready for something more advanced and looking to invest in private markets.

(Name of customer) is a (specific number)-year-old tech worker who felt like he had his portfolio figured out but wanted to see what other options were available to him without hiring a wealth manager. He ended up using (Startup), an app that takes a much lower fee and opens access to investments that are typically only available to the rich via a network of advisors, think hedge funds, VC, and private equity.

(Name of customer) used (Startup) to become an accredited investor and invest in AI-powered portfolios and private credit opportunities. Would you be interested in speaking with him? I can also offer an interview with (Startup)'s co-founder, (name of co-founder), to discuss why he and (oddly large number) of his former (big startup name) colleagues launched (Startup).

I like the "two for one" approach in this pitch, using a real customer as well as a trend to hook the reporter. As mentioned, "plating a story" helps a journalist see and receive all aspects of a potential story. Related to trends but far faster in terms of pitching speed is "newsjacking."

NEWSJACKING

A lot of news happens in a flurry. It's the nature of news in today's world, and you can use this to your advantage if you and your PR team are lightning fast, usually moving within hours. Let's look at an example, which landed on NBC:

Subject Line: Data for (reporter's name): Economic Impact of Hurricane Beryl on Houston Metropolitan Area

Hi XX,

Reaching out to see if you'd be interested in an analysis on the economic impact of Hurricane Beryl in Houston from (Startup), a (description of Startup):

(Startup) analyzed the economic impact repair costs would have on the Houston area and found:

- Assuming one hundred thousand people in the Houston metro area were not able to work for just one week following the hurricane, the total loss in output would be $1.3 billion.
- Repairing the damage will support over 102,000 jobs, with $6.9 billion in labor income and $9.9 billion in contribution to GDP.
- Through the supply chain and household spending, repairs will support over eighty-eight thousand jobs, with $5.9 billion in labor income, and $10.9 billion in contribution to GDP.

You can read their full 2024 hurricane season analysis here (link included), and I can also arrange an interview with (name), (Startup)'s chief economist and data officer, if you're interested in discussing the data further. Let me know!

Numbers were key to this pitch as well as a morning-of pitch following the end of this awful hurricane.

BYLINES

A trickier but equally valuable piece of coverage you may be able to secure is a byline, an article written by you (or your PR team) that a media outlet decides to publish. Some media outlets, like *Fast Company* and *Harvard Business Review*, take "contributed content," and other outlets, such as *The New York Times* and *The Wall Street Journal*, take more opinionated pieces called "editorials." I say "tricker" because you don't often pitch a journalist or editor with an idea for a byline but rather submit a full piece, usually on a direct-submission form at the news outlet.

PODCASTS

Podcasts are great for practicing your messaging and having longer-form conversations with "hosts" who are usually not journalists. That said, many newsrooms now produce one, if not several, of their own podcasts, and anything you say digitally, whether on a podcast produced by a casual expert or a national media outlet, can be dug up on the internet somewhere. Here's one pitch that secured an interview on one of *Fortune*'s podcasts:

> Subject Line: Re: Podcast Guest? How (Major Bank) Is Working with a Digital Family Office
>
> Hey XX,
>
> Wanted to see if you'd be interested in speaking with (founder), co-founder, and CEO of (Startup).
>
> Traditional banking companies like (major bank) are looking to modernize their wealth management offerings by working with (Startup), a (description of the Startup). The company is paving the way by

showing people can grow, manage, and protect their wealth with less paperwork via (a technology).

What do you think? (Founder) would love to be a guest on your podcast, but he's also open to an intro call if you'd like to learn more on background.

About (Startup): (Startup) was founded by (fancy tech place) employees who left to build a (technology) that is dedicated to extending the financial superpowers of the (certain audience). (Startup) launched in (year) with $XM in funding, with investments from (big VC fund), (big VC fund), and (big VC fund).

I love this pitch because it doesn't even start with a full sentence. It gets right into the founder being teed up, leverages a notable brand name the startup works with, and offers a quick and impressive boilerplate about the startup itself so the journalist doesn't even need to click around further.

We've covered a lot of pitches, and this list was not exhaustive. I hope this chapter has conveyed how many *kinds* of news moments can convert into media coverage. With considered (for your customers, sensitive data, and so on) creativity and elbow grease, you should never find yourself with "no stories" to pitch the media, unless you are a pre-seed or seed-stage founder who hasn't yet secured customers, case studies, data, funding, and the like. Pitching is just one key part of securing media coverage, however. The other is acing the media interview, so let's get to that.

CHAPTER 4 SUMMARY POINTS

- Your new office dog or new office space are not pitches a journalist will likely cover.
- Funding, expert sources, customers, reports and data, trends, newsjacking, bylines, and podcast pitches can be of interest to the media, but this is not an exhaustive list.
- Anyone can pitch a journalist. The reason you use PR professionals is because they should know journalists and how to pitch them.

Chapter 5

Acing Media Interviews

It's time to stick the landing. Your startup is doing (relatively) well, you have your messaging down pat, and a journalist has scheduled a time to talk or meet with you because a pitch that you or your PR team sent was opened and responded to, which is rare, as you now know. Before you envision how great it's going to be to send your team, VCs, and mom an article all about how super your venture-backed startup is, you first need to nail the media interview.

A media interview isn't like a job interview at your startup or a pitch at a VC fund. Usually, several rounds of interviews or pitches take place for a job or funding, assuming that you or a candidate continues to impress the parties that be. Media interviews are instead often one and done, with the rare exceptions of long-form or investigative stories. See Chapter 6 for media personas, such as Sleuthy Sally, who is usually trying to dig for a story—and not a flattering one, to be sure.

Given the one-and-done nature of media interviews, the stakes are higher, so you need to get both feet firmly on the ground to "stick the landing." A poor media interview can result in no coverage at all simply because you were boring or confusing. A really poor media interview results in quotes you're not pleased to read (but said) or a headline that's negative (but accurate). This is where media training comes into play. Media training is simply learning a kind of communication that can help you to better interact with media, and good media training often leads to consistent brand messaging, polished quotes, and fewer unwanted surprises in media coverage. I'm going to cover several techniques and tips in this chapter, but media training needs to be experienced firsthand and often. It also gets dismissed a lot. Before we get into any of the techniques then, I have to share a few common pushbacks I hear from venture-backed founders who want to ditch media training:

COMMON "I DON'T NEED MEDIA TRAINING" REMARKS

"BUT I PITCH MY COMPANY ALL THE TIME"

This is the standard response from founders. Though VCs will poke holes and ask challenging questions, they often do not run on deadlines like journalists do. Three-hour-long interviews with a journalist, for instance, are rare, and journalists aren't sending carefully crafted deal memos to their colleagues like a VC would. In addition, journalists are looking for succinct sound bites, phrases and statements that can drop neatly into an online piece or work well on a live, five-minute TV spot. I've often heard founders take fourteen minutes to answer, "What does your startup do?" That's too long an answer for a journalist, as we covered in Chapter 2 about messaging. Media training will help you condense narratives into the sound bites journalists need.

BUT I'M ALREADY WELL SPOKEN AND COMFORTABLE SPEAKING IN FRONT OF TONS OF PEOPLE

Here's another common dismissal from founders who are polished on stages and panels. You can command a room, finish a fifteen-minute TEDx Talk without a flub, and banter on a panel in front of a thousand people, sure. While these skills are great, they can be refined for one-on-one exchanges with journalists. Interviews with the media are not staged or written speeches. Rather, media interviews can sound more like interrogations as journalists dig for an opinion or angle to support their particular stories. Media training can further enhance a good speaker's ability to block, bridge, or flag key messages, which we'll get into later in this chapter.

But It's Just an Interview to Learn More About Us

A journalist is not your friend, and they don't want to be your friend. We'll talk about this in Chapter 6, particularly with Buddy Bill, who seems so nice. There are exceptions, of course, but overall, journalists seek interviews to capture perspectives and information to create their stories. A journalist may indicate that an interview is on background or exploratory, but that shouldn't be taken as a cue to be casual. Though media relations is about relationship building, you and your spokespersons need to tread lightly when it comes to this, as excessive comfort can lead you to share details you may wish you hadn't.

BUT I'VE BEEN DOING THIS FOR TWENTY YEARS

Being well versed in an industry can backfire because of jargon. An executive who uses too many industry terms or acronyms or who name drops can leave some media baffled or disinterested. While there are plenty of journalists with deep expertise in specific industries, like Expert Elaine, whom we'll meet in Chapter

6, media training can help you simplify key messages so jargon doesn't become a distraction.

BUT I DID MEDIA TRAINING TWO YEARS AGO

If it's been several months, a refresher doesn't hurt. Media training, like most skills, is only refined with practice. The only exception to this retort is if you are constantly being interviewed and practicing with the media on a weekly or more frequent basis.

Hopefully, you're now on board to do media training, which your PR agency, freelance publicist, or the PR person at one of your VC funds should be able to handle once you get to that point. Let's turn now to how to prep, perform, and perfect media interviews, a big aspect of "sticking the landing" and becoming a Flack Fairy.

PREPARE

Just like a pitch to a VC, you'll want to do some homework before your interview. Here are the steps to best prepare for your media interview:

RESPOND AND BOOK THE INTERVIEW

First things first: Make sure to respond to the media's request ASAP and get a time confirmed. If you have a PR agency or freelance publicist working with you, then this is their number-one function as a conduit to the media, and they should be telling you about media responses in real time. If you're receiving a journalist's request directly, though, then be consistent and respond directly, looping in the appropriate PR team if they're in place. Speed wins with the media, and you don't want to be passed over for commentary because your competitors hopped right on a request if the objective is clearly stated. If you're a bit tepid or unsure of what a journalist wants, check with your PR team immediately or directly ask what the interview entails and what the deadline is. Most journalists include their timeframes in response to a pitch or need for a story, such as, "I'm filing this story by 5:00 p.m. PT today, so I need any commentary about X by 2:00 p.m. PT," or, "I'm working on a story about Y, which I have to submit by EOW. Let me know if you have time tomorrow for a call."

FOLLOW

Next, follow the journalist you'll be speaking with on LinkedIn. Instagram, TikTok, and X are a bit touchier and less preferred, but do a quick search to see if the journalist showcases their professional life on these platforms. Read up on the journalist's posts, though there's no need to be a stalker and like or comment on every one.

READ

In addition to scrolling any online posts from the journalist, do a full read of the last three to five articles the journalist wrote. What's the tone of the articles? Does the journalist like to drop in a lot of quotes? See if you can deduce a pattern of preferences or style.

GATHER

A journalist isn't talking with you out of boredom. There's an angle to the story or a potential one that the journalist is seeking. If it's not clear what the story is about, ask. If the journalist is responding to a particular pitch, then you're likely to know the angle, but it doesn't hurt to clarify with something like, "I'm excited to talk with you at 2:00 p.m. ET today about X. Is there anything else you'd like to cover about X during our twenty minutes that I may prepare for? Otherwise, I'll see you on Zoom per our calendar invite." You may not get a response ahead of the interview, and that's okay.

GET CLEAR

Remember that messaging doc? Take a read, say it out loud a few times, and practice it, if possible, with a colleague who can act like a journalist if your PR team isn't in place or around. Better yet, if the interview is not in person, print out your messaging doc so you have a quick cheat sheet you can reference. If you know the context of the interview, have a few notes jotted down as well.

PERFORM

Now, you're in the hot seat, speaking with the journalist. I'll cover different settings in a moment, but these performance tips work across all settings, from on-camera or in-studio interviews to phone calls.

KEEP RESPONSES TO 120 SECONDS

Journalists need sound bites, not diatribes. There are no four-paragraph-long quotes in news articles or twenty-two-minute TV segments based on a single answer. Succinctness is sadly not the strong suit of many founders. I get it: You are enthralled and excited by what you're building, but you need to master the grace and power of shutting up. Practice answers while timing yourself with 120 seconds on the clock. It's the journalist's job to ask you the questions, so let them.

USE EVERYDAY LANGUAGE

Unless you're speaking with Expert Elaine, whom we'll meet in Chapter 6, it's important to use simple language that clearly conveys what you're building and why. I'm not saying you need to "dumb down" your message if you're a particularly technical startup. Rather, make sure your smart mom would understand what you're saying.

SPEAK LOUDLY

Have you ever seen a soft-spoken news anchor? You haven't. That's because crisp audio is essential to a good interview. You don't want to be misquoted because your interview on the phone went poorly as you were whispering in the broom closet of a conference hall. Nor do you want your live TV interview to be botched because the sound guys had to dial up your mic in live time.

BE OKAY WITH SILENCE

As mentioned, it's the journalist's job to ask you the questions. During an interview that is not live, a reporter may be taking notes. Let the clicking of the keyboard continue until they catch up. In a live interview, allow the journalist to do their job and tee up their next question.

DON'T KNOW IT ALL

Plenty of research has shown that saying, "I don't know," can foster trust. Whether you believe the research or not, this much seems true: Someone so dead set on claiming to know everything is not to be trusted. If a journalist asks you something you don't know the answer to, bridge to something you do know: "I don't know the details about X, but what I do know is Z." We'll cover bridging later in this chapter.

SHARE STORIES

Facts tell, but stories sell, as we covered in Chapter 4. Come to an interview with two or three stories from your customers that beautifully showcase the reason your startup exists. "We've changed the lives of more than two thousand patients," is not as compelling as, "We've changed the lives of more than two thousand patients, and I'd like to share a story about Sarah, one of our customers, who is now alive because of the treatment she received from us last year..."

PERFECT

You completed the interview—phew. Your job isn't completely done though. A few extra steps will better your next interview as well as possibly help the one you just did.

ASK

A reporter is constantly collecting sources, data, and details. It doesn't hurt to ask a journalist if there's anything you can provide them for the story you were just interviewed for or for something in the future. Introductions to hard-to-contact folks can be particularly valuable. For VCs, it's their limited partners. For founders like you, it may be a celebrity investor, a board member who chairs other organizations, or an official in a public office. If you can save a journalist time, then you'll earn a spot on a journalist's short list of contacts to call.

THANK

Maybe the journalist was told or assigned to talk with you, or perhaps the interview was a bit dicey because it was hard-hitting. That doesn't mean you can't be gracious in thanking the journalist for their time and attention. This is similar to pitching VCs who turn you down. Time is valuable, so anyone who gives you some should be thanked.

DON'T ASK FOR A PEEK

I still hear of founders asking journalists to see a copy of an article ahead of it going live. This is a total rookie ask, like asking a VC to sign an NDA before a pitch. It's just not done, and you'll look silly in making such a request.

SHARE

Assuming the article or piece that got published based on your interview is favorable, make sure you share it on social media. LinkedIn is one of the best places on the internet right now to do so and gives journalists public acknowledgment of their work. That said, keep it professional, as you're not friends with the journalist, which we'll cover in Chapter 6.

REVIEW

You can always improve. Ideally right after the interview, do a self-audit on what you aced and what could have been improved. If you had someone listening in, like your PR freelancer, push for specific feedback. For our clients, if we attend the call, we discuss feedback right after an interview and include the points we covered in an email as well, just to hammer home the recommendations.

Now you've prepped, performed, and perfected your media interview skills overall. Like most things, the more reps you do, the easier the interviews will become. That said, don't get lazy. Resist cutting corners, such as not reviewing a journalist's work ahead of an interview or not thanking a journalist after a good story because you got busy.

INTERVIEW TIPS FOR IN-PERSON, TV, PHONE, OR VIDEO CONFERENCE INTERVIEWS

There are some nuances to the formats media interviews take, however basic they may sound. Take a quick read of the tips below so you don't become part of a compilation of YouTube clips labeled "failed media interviews: WATCH NOW." These tips can be used in addition to the ones we covered above in the Prepare, Perform, and Perfect sections.

IN PERSON

I love being in person. Being in person grants you the full array of verbal and nonverbal communication. Use this to your advantage, and take cues from body language. Is the reporter sitting up stick straight or hunched over a laptop, four inches from the screen? Consider being more formal in the former situation, and lean in toward the reporter in the latter to mirror behavior. Mirroring has long been shown to help establish trust and empathy.

TV

A live TV spot is the varsity level of media interviews. If you're going to a studio where the interview is taking place, get there thirty minutes before the producer said you should arrive. You don't want to be rushing to get on set, frazzled and sweaty. No one can wipe your forehead in the middle of a live segment.

Clothing-wise, it's a good idea to avoid patterned clothing and solid, bright white. Patterns can be distracting, and bright white can blow out your features. Founders sometimes ask, "Well, I never wear a dress, so do I need to?" or, "I just don't put on jackets and a tie. Should I?" Wear what's you, but as when you go to church, the beach, or the White House, attire is communication.

When the interview is rolling, there's even more for you to consider. First, keep your eyes on the reporter. You're talking with the reporter, not with a camera. This trips up a lot of people as they panic, trying to look into various cameras, searching for the "face" to talk to. The reporter is the face. The exception to this is if you're conducting a live TV segment from, say, your office, and you're doing it via your laptop. In this case, you'll want to look into the camera of your laptop.

Second, if you're seated in one of those godforsaken swivel chairs, keep your feet on the ground to avoid moving back and forth. Some people tamper nerves by swinging around in these chairs, but then their message gets completely thrown out the window because of the distraction. Lastly, and also related to nerves, watch yourself for excessive nodding, blinking, or fiddling.

PHONE

A phone interview sounds low key compared to a live TV spot, and it is to some extent. You can take advantage of the nonvisual format by having your messaging right in front of you for quick reference. Make sure not to read it stiffly to avoid sounding canned. If you want, you can stand up and assume a power pose if that gives you a feeling of confidence.[23]

---

23   Debate is still ongoing about the significance of standing in such a position, but why not do so if it helps?; Tom Loncar, "A Decade of Power Posing: Where Do We Stand?," *The Psychologist*, June 8, 2021, https://www.bps.org.uk/psychologist/decade-power-posing-where-do-we-stand.

VIDEO CONFERENCING

Video conferencing doesn't seem to be going away anytime soon. Some journalists prefer the visual component of a video call on Zoom, Google Meet, Teams, or whatnot. If your interview will take place via video call, make sure you're first familiar with the platform you'll be joining by testing out the link before the interview. I always seem to get a software update right before a webinar or big pitch, for instance.

Lighting and sound are also not to be overlooked, as simple as it sounds. You don't want to look like you're in a jail cell with echoing sound and glaring fluorescent lighting that casts shadows down on your face. "But who cares?" you may ask. Any distraction from your messaging is a potential problem, so why risk it? Make sure your headphones (yes, cords) are working seamlessly and that good lighting is in place.

BLOCKING, BRIDGING, AND FLAGGING

You've nailed your messaging so far and are feeling more comfortable with journalists. Excellent! You're leaps and bounds ahead of most venture-backed startup founders because few practice their messaging with reporters to perfect it. In this section, I'll cover a few advanced techniques you can hone to enhance your media interviews.

BLOCKING

Blocking is exactly what it sounds like. It's a response to a journalist's question that shuts down the inquiry and asserts a boundary. You're not likely to pull out a block if you're an early-stage founder talking about a Series B funding round, which is pretty standard stuff, but as you get into your later stages, blocking may be needed to deter questions about going public, conducting layoffs, doing a down round, working with certain industry players, and so on. Blocking sounds like the following:

"I can't answer that, but what I can tell you is..."

"The bigger question at stake is..."

"As I said, I will not discuss the details of X. I can discuss..."

BRIDGING

Bridging helps you get from one point to another you'd much rather talk about. Think of bridging as holding your hand out, stretching to grasp the wrist of the journalist, and saying, "Let's go over here." A journalist's job is to get the information needed for a story, but your job is to convey the messages of your startup successfully, and bridging can help you get your job done with grace. Bridging examples include:

"I'd like to add..."

"Another aspect to consider in the context of X is..."

"That's a good point, and your audience may further want to understand..."

FLAGGING

Flags are for emphasis. A journalist will usually ask at the end of an interview (live TV interviews excluded), "Is there anything you'd like to add?" That's a layup for a flag where you can respond, "I'd like to emphasize X..." Don't be afraid to be the PR version of a CRO, which is not a chief revenue officer but rather a chief repeating officer. Here are a few example phrases for flags:

"As I said earlier..."

"It's important that I emphasize..."

"I want to highlight again..."

"Remember, the mission of our startup is..."

"ON THE RECORD," "OFF THE RECORD," AND "ON BACKGROUND"

I can't tell you how many times we've heard a founder complain about a quote that a journalist included in an article. To be clear, the founder said the exact words published. (We know this because we were staffing the interview too.) "But I thought the interview was over," a founder will say, or, "We were just chatting about something totally unrelated in the bathroom line!" I know, but you need to assume everything you say to a journalist, however casually, is on the record. The exception is if a reporter explicitly confirms your commentary is off the record or just on background.

Let's cover the distinction between "off the record" and "on background" to be certain it's clear. "Off the record" means whatever you say is just between you and the journalist. Your name, other names you dropped, your words, and so on are not to be included in an article or piece the journalist completes. "On background" is a bit different: Nothing will be attributed to you specifically, but the information you share can be reported by the journalist. When an article cites "a company spokesperson" or "people familiar with the situation," this is a clue that "on background" interviews were conducted.

Unfortunately, there's no official form, like an employee contract or a nondisclosure agreement, that a reporter signs to pledge your anonymity, but in all the years we've worked with journalists, we haven't seen a reporter forget that you were off the record or on background. Any situation that requires an off-the-record or on-background request usually pertains to a sensitive or investigative story that you likely don't want to be part of.

There are many aspects to consider when talking with the media, as we've covered in this chapter. First, do media training and do it often, no matter how "good" you believe you already are. Then, practice, practice, practice your interview skills so you can seamlessly bridge, block, and flag messages as you speak with the media. The next part of becoming a dangerous and dominating Flack Fairy is anticipating some media types you may meet as you achieve earned media.

CHAPTER 5 SUMMARY POINTS

- Don't "wing it": Getting fully prepared for a media interview will help prevent headlines and quotes you aren't happy with. Prepare, perform, and perfect.
- Like pitching VCs, practicing media interviews takes reps. Make sure you do media training.
- As you get better, you can lean on media interview skills like bridging, blocking, and flagging.

Chapter 6

Taking on Media Personas

Like VCs and founders, journalists have all sorts of personalities and traits. And like VCs and founders, journalists fall into tropes. You'll likely meet many of them as you build your venture-backed startup and pursue earned media over the years. If you're lucky enough to grow your venture-backed startup into a unicorn, you'll absolutely meet journalists because you'll simply be at a level subject to the media sniffing around, whether you prefer it or not. This chapter outlines a few common media types you may encounter as well as specific suggestions on how to work with them that expand beyond the advice given in Chapter 5.

One important thing to note before we get into any of these media personas is this: journalists are curious, dogged people. They aren't doing journalism for an easy life. Hundreds of journalists are in jail around the world at any given moment, and layoffs are a constant reality in newsrooms.[24] Journalists don't relent; they

---

24 Check out Reporters Without Borders or the Committee to Protect Journalists, two nonprofits that track and advocate for journalists' safety.

push for truth and transparency, and they dig for as many facts as feasible. They aren't doing their jobs for the money either. A few will write books and hope for a bestseller or podcast deal, though much like teachers, social workers, and others who try to keep the whole of society just and good, journalists are often called to their professions. I offer this as a reminder to you, a venture-backed founder and Flack Fairy in the making, so you keep this context in mind when interacting with any journalist. They're doing a difficult job with a clear calling, like you. But unlike you, they're likely not going to see a fat salary or a life-changing payday at some point.

Here are a few common media types you may meet along the way as you secure earned media and build your venture-backed startup.

BUDDY BILL

Buddy Bill is friendly, even eager, like a golden retriever. "He's so nice," you think. "He's so into our story!" You smile, but Buddy Bill is just into everyone. Buddy Bills are the kinds of journalists agencies love to work with as well. They send us little emails like, "The story will go live tomorrow, FYI," or, "Just fact-checking the piece right now. Will keep you posted if another interview is needed." The caution with Buddy Bill is to remember he's not your friend, never was, and never should be unless he steps out of journalism and goes to a startup like yours or the "dark side," public relations. A friend shows you grace and compassion. He nods along and says, "Yeah, that's really rough. Sorry you're going through that." A journalist, even Buddy Bill, has a job to do. He will quote you in a piece because you said it in an interview. You didn't know you were having an interview? Buddy Bill was recording the call, but you forgot. Or worse, you thought you were friends.

The best approach with Buddy Bill is to not get too cozy. Simply remember you both have a job to do. Yours is to convey your story well, and Buddy Bill's is to turn in a good story.

TERSE TERRI

Terse Terri definitely doesn't want to be your friend; that much is clear. She's on a deadline, maybe has twelve minutes for you for an interview, and doesn't want a follow-up from you or any PR person. "Oooof," you may sigh. But Terse Terri is often just under pressure and isn't digging for details for her assignment, unlike Sleuthy Sally (below). It's not personal, and you weren't expecting an invite to her birthday party next weekend anyway.

Terse Terri may interrupt you, quickly shift to another topic, and speak quickly. All of this is fine. Your best bet in dealing with Terse Terri is to deliver your message in a crisp and clear way. Match the tone of urgency as well and ask if there is anything you said that needs more clarity or if you can provide her with more information via email right away.

SLEUTHY SALLY

Sleuthy Sally is sniffing around, and she thinks you're holding a bag of treats. Her interviews tend to be meandering and slow because the direction of the interview isn't perhaps fully known, even to Sleuthy Sally. The question, "What does she even want?" may float through your mind.

You're more likely to meet a Sleuthy Sally if you're becoming a big deal. If you've secured eyebrow-raising rounds of capital, laid off hundreds of people, pissed off regulators or other legacy entities in your space, or gotten heaps of media attention because your PR agency is killing it and you are too, be ready to meet Sleuthy Sally. For positive or negative reasons, becoming a big deal is blood in the water for the shark known as Sleuthy Sally. That said, Sleuthy Sally doesn't typically pay attention to seed or early-stage startups. It's really not an interest to Sleuthy Sally if you shed five of your fifteen employees because you need to extend your runway as a Series A startup. There is a benefit to being too small in this case.

Your best defense before you meet Sleuthy Sally is to have your PR army in place and on alert. Some in-house PR teams and even PR agencies are notorious for shielding founders and C-suite executives from Sleuthy Sally. Great publicists, after all, are as well versed in landing a mountain of media coverage as they are in ensuring absolutely zero is mentioned in the media. On a positive note, Sleuthy Sally is often as easy to spot as a shark in six feet of clear water. As discussed in Chapter 5, about acing media interviews, if you read up on Sleuthy Sally and note that her last nine stories had an investigative tone or a halting headline, then you know you're putting yourself in the shark's house. Some Sleuthy Sallys are even more obvious via their bylines or authors' bios. "Investigative reporter," or, "So-and-so is part of the media outlet's investigative team," are hallmarks of a Sleuthy Sally. Proceed with caution, unlike with Clueless Chad.

CLUELESS CHAD

Poor Chad. He just started his beat a month ago and has no clue about the EVcharging ecosystem, ML applications in medicine, or synthetic data for AI testing. But someone gave him an assignment, and he needs to turn in a story. To be clear, Clueless Chad is not dumb, as every journalist is whip sharp as a function of surviving their tough career. "Wow. I am starting at square one here," is a typical response to Clueless Chad.

The best approach to Clueless Chad is to use his lack of knowledge as an opportunity. You know everything about your industry, and here's someone who is desperate to know anything about it. Come with the patience of a great teacher and you'll go far with Clueless Chad, who will likely come back to you as a reliable source, particularly if you can break down complex aspects about your field.

One point on Clueless Chad though. The journalist you are speaking with may appear to be a Clueless Chad but in fact may be a Sleuthy Sally or Expert Elaine in disguise. As a good rule, just assume every reporter is a Sleuthy Sally and be on defense at all times.

EXPERT ELAINE

Expert Elaine has been covering your industry since you were in high school. She has two PhDs and doesn't care about the one you got from some non–Ivy League school. Some founders love Expert Elaine because it's delightful to meet a journalist, or really anyone, at your level of niche expertise who can nerd out with you. "Finally!" you think. While you can get right into it with Expert Elaine, remember she likely knows everyone and everything you're about to tee up. Trying to gloss over a company or person who is associated with your startup in some way, like claiming so-and-so is an "advisor" of your startup, will be fact-checked. She's probably texting the person you named right now in fact.

Expert Elaine is often a cornerstone in your industry. You're going to see her at industry events, on panels, on awards committees, and so on. As she is inescapable, your best bet is to earn her respect and regard so you can be the first one she texts when she needs a reliable source who doesn't BS her.

QUESTIONER QUINTEN

Questioner Quinten is an eager beaver. He may be spun up about all the questions he just needs to get out and ask or he may be one of those journalists who loves to talk more than listen. A prompt from Questioner Quinten sounds like, "So last year, you closed $40 million from that venture fund, and you've hired thirty-two people since then. What are you now focused on, and how are all those employees fairing in this tough labor market? And, oh yeah, I heard from a source you may be hiring a new CTO from a competitor? What can you say about that? And then we can get into the federal thing Congress just passed that likely impacts your industry, or does it?" To Questioner Quinten, this is his first question. "Okkkkkkkayyy," you're thinking.

The best defense to Questioner Quinten is documentation. Jot down all the questions Questioner Quinten throws your way and clarify them one by one. This slows down the (often unintended) assault and ensures you get to every question. If there aren't too many in one breath, you can restate and reorder them: "Those are a lot of good questions you bring up, Quinten. First, let me address the question about the employee market and then the CTO hire…"

The list above of journalist tropes isn't comprehensive but identifies a few of the kinds we've seen over the years. I've included a quick cheat-sheet summary below to sum up the types for easy reference. In the next chapter, we'll get into another realm of PR where the media often live or have influence: awards and speaking opportunities.

Media persona	How to spot	Best approach
Buddy Bill	seems like a friend	don't get too cozy
Terse Terri	seems in a rush	keep your message crisp and clear
Sleuthy Sally	seems like a spy	be on alert
Clueless Chad	seems overwhelmed	get in teacher mode
Expert Elaine	seems to know everyone in your space	don't name-drop unless you want to be checked
Questioner Quinten	seems hyper	document and address every question

CHAPTER 6 SUMMARY POINTS

- Journalists have their jobs to do, and you have your job of conveying your startup's messaging clearly and persuasively.
- All kinds of journalists exist; get familiar with a few of the common tropes to better prepare yourself.

Chapter 7

Winning Awards and Speaking Opportunities

We have the media well covered at this point, but we still have many chapters to get through before you can become a Flack Fairy. This chapter pertains to awards and speaking opportunities. They aren't as flashy or often as coveted as top-tier media placements, but awards as well as speaking opportunities can round out a solid PR campaign. Here's why: Awards and evidence of your stage presence enhance the story of your startup to your VCs, talent, customers, industry influencers, and even the media themselves. I know some of you are reading this chapter and feeling, "There's more? Now I need to get on some stage or get some award?" Yes, Flack Fairy, there's more. You certainly don't have to do awards and stages, but if you have the bandwidth and a team that can line up the opportunities and beat down the ones that aren't high quality, awards and speaking can be valuable. You can think of media placements as a cake and awards and panel opportunities as some icing with rainbow sprinkles. Rainbow sprinkles don't hurt, and most people love them.

Let me emphasize the "team" part of the previous paragraph. I'm sure you know what I'm about to say: Yep, winning awards and speaking opportunities takes work, just like securing great media coverage. Some of the most prestigious awards, like *Time* magazine's TIME100 list or CNBC's Disruptor 50 list, entail several interviews after the application. Other speaking opportunities, such as *The Wall Street Journal*'s Future of Everything Festival or the TechCrunch Disrupt conference, require all kinds of preparation for a thirty-minute panel. Assuming you're down for the work, take a look at the best tips to nab the awards and get on a stage.

CONTACT THE ORGANIZERS

Most startups or PR agencies will contact awards or panel organizers *after* submission. Do the opposite. Make inroads and develop relationships with any awards or speaking organizers months in advance of the submission forms even opening. The benefit of this proactive approach is that it helps you garner details that may not be so apparent on a form or website link. For instance, some awards and panels push their deadlines by a week or two. Others waive fees for certain circumstances. In other cases, you can get close to the team in charge of selecting winning nominations and gather insights on their pet peeves or turnoffs. It doesn't hurt to make contact well in advance of a submission.

One note on fees while we're here: A lot of awards have some fee, usually a few hundred dollars, associated with submission. Don't be put off by this. Media organizations have found award fees to be one way to supplement their shrinking P&Ls. If awards are going to be part of your PR push, consider adding in a budget of $3,000 to $10,000 a year just for award submissions. On the other hand, speaking opportunities often do not have a fee associated with submission, but you'll usually have to pay your way to get to the event. The exception is if you're some megawatt startup founder who has a speaking bureau agent. In that case, organizers pay *you* to come to their events. There are also events that allow a "pay to play" kind of ticket. One founder we represented forked over $100,000 to gain a spot on a stage at an event known to host the who's who of the billionaire bunch.

SUSS OUT PREVIOUS WINNERS OR SPEAKERS

You need to determine what "league" you're competing in. Who was on stage at the previous event? Which companies were showcased on the last couple lists? It's disappointing for some startup founders to hear this, but sometimes a startup just isn't at the level yet to apply for an award or speaking opportunity. Of course, most startups love a challenge, but first, compare yourself to previous winners or speakers to assess your likelihood of winning an award or securing a speaking spot.

Consider how real estate agents use comparables (comps) to see what homes or apartments have sold for in the neighborhoods where they're getting ready to sell. A good real estate agent prices a home in the ballpark of what a reasonable buyer would go for, using the comps as supporting evidence. Similarly, we use panel and award comps with our startups. If an award list only features public and later-stage startups with at least a thousand employees, then a startup with ten employees that is just finding its momentum likely has a super slim chance of winning. It's not impossible, but do you want to win or not?

CHECK THE QUESTIONS AHEAD OF TIME

Even if you know the organizers and feel you have a decent chance of nabbing a coveted award or speaking slot, check what is required for the panel or award submission. Some forms may take an hour to complete, while others could require input from several departments and team leads. In addition, some submissions require sensitive information, such as revenue or employee hiring figures, and you may not be open to sharing that information just yet.

USE HARD DATA TO BACK UP YOUR CLAIMS

Let's say you're well aware of what is required for an award or speaking submission form and are ready to cross it off the list. In fact, you have your startup's messaging and marketing materials right in hand and can't wait to tell the award or speaking committee how your startup is the "first," "biggest," and "best in class" startup practically ever. None of these adjectives matter unless you can prove to the committee, with hard and specific data, how you back up your audacious claims. "Our startup grew 30 percent last year and helped solve the crisis of loneliness in America with our product launch last May," is weak compared to, "Our startup exceeded $18 million in revenue last year and was used by more than 2,500 physicians who are aligned with our mission of ending loneliness in America."

TELL COMPELLING STORIES

As the adage goes, "Facts tell, but stories sell." Now take your hard data and stats and match them with a few choice stories that beautifully convey the impact your startup is making. Customer quotes, testimonials, and narratives are what you're looking for in as much detail as feasible. Compelling one-liners ("This startup utterly changed my relationship with my six-year-old," for example) and detailed journeys of how your startup touched real people are compelling complements to strong data. Stories told via your customers are also third-party validation. Make sure to get explicit permission from anyone if you're going to use real names.

BE BRIEF

This is the hardest and most unintuitive tip. If a certain question on an award or speaking form has a word limit of five hundred, there is no need to write 497 words. Nearly all our successful submissions have clocked in at around *half* the word limit. This quote from Blaise Pascal rings true: "The present letter is a very long one, simply because I had no leisure to make it shorter."[25] Take the time to be concise.

Winning awards and speaking engagements requires a thoughtful and measured approach that takes work. When you secure them, though, they often *aid* you in seizing top-tier media because of the validation they signal. To be clear: Winning an award or getting on a panel is not a story a journalist is typically going to write about. Rather, when you rack up awards and presence on stages, your clout as an industry leader rises.

Now, did you get that award or dazzle on stage? Excellent. Don't let such a win go without some marketing and sales enablement. I cover this in Chapter 12 about making a media flywheel. Before we get into the fun of that material, though, let's cover a big aspect of public relations that isn't fun but is always looming: crisis communications.

---

25 Blaise Pascal, *The Provincial Letters*, trans. Thomas M'Crie, ed. O. W. Wight (Hurd and Houghton, 1866), 417.

CHAPTER 7 SUMMARY POINTS

- Awards and speaking engagements are another tool in your PR tool kit to signal to your audiences why your venture-backed startup matters.

- Unlike a pitch, which you can quickly shoot off to a journalist's inbox, awards and speaking opportunities usually require significantly more time and effort.

- Some awards require fees, and speaking opportunities may not cover your travel. Consider a budget if you're adding awards and speaking engagements to your PR mix.

Chapter 8

Avoiding a Crisis

No one likes insurance, estate planning, and prenups, and the same is true for crisis-communications planning. Crisis communications is absolutely part of being dangerous and dominating as a Flack Fairy, as un-fun as this stuff is. If your venture-backed startup is at or beyond a Series A, you're likely big enough to get into some crisis moments that require swift communication. I know you want to protest. You're building an enterprise AI tool that's for nerdy CTOs or have an application related to material coating for chips. What could happen that anyone would care about? My response: Have you met people? It's hardly a question. I know you have met people, and people get wound up about everything. From photos of Nazi-alluding underwear posted on a website to a sexual harassment allegation made at lunch about a hot dog, I've seen and dealt with all kinds of lapses in judgment that balloon into crises.

In this chapter, I'll cover what a crisis is and various crisis levels, the basics of a crisis-communications flow, crisis scenario planning, and a method for considering emerging crises that you may or may not want to comment on.

DEFINING A PR CRISIS AND ITS LEVEL

A startup will deal with many crises. The good news is that most are not PR crises that require an immediate and swift response. For instance, you're having a supply chain crisis, and a chip you need may not arrive in time for Q4 shipments, more than a year away. Or Slack is down on Monday morning, and your team is stuck on email and Zoom for a few hours. These are annoying situations, not even crises, and you're not going to need a multi-step communications plan.

Rather, a PR crisis that requires you to act usually has one of the following elements: a risk to public safety, possible financial loss, or reputational damage. Put another way, if you answer yes to any of the following three questions, you'll need to get moving on a PR crisis plan:

- Are the lives or safety of the people we work with, such as clients, the team, or our investors, in jeopardy? Example: You have employees who need to evacuate due to an incoming hurricane.
- Does this situation impact our financial standing? Example: You have to conduct layoffs or complete a down round of financing.
- Could this situation hurt our reputation in any way? Example: Your startup leaks the personal banking information of millions of users.

Let's now look at the three levels at which a PR crisis could be brewing. The first is a low level: There's not much risk to safety, finances, or reputation. At this low level, stakeholders are not even aware of the situation or it's so minor that nothing is mentioned. You may get a few rumblings from, say, customers, but for the time being, the situation is at a low intensity. At this level, the best course of action is passive observation: Don't take your eyes off it, but there's no need to swing into action.

Next is a moderate level: Not only do you have internal stakeholders talking about the situation, but now external stakeholders are murmuring. Perhaps you've had a reporter or curious regulator in your space email the PR team. The situation is escalating but not at a full-blown crisis. At this stage, you need to be monitoring the situation with active observation: Multiple people close to the situation should be watching it 24/7. You should dust off your crisis-communications plan, which we'll cover below, and get it rolling.

The last level of a PR crisis is high. Now you're dealing with a slew of internal and external stakeholders' communications. The media is emailing you, customers are tagging you on social media, and employees are chattering on Slack at a speedy clip. You're in a full PR crisis now, and your PR crisis-communications plan should be well under way. Let's now look at the five main stages of a communications plan.

THE FIVE STEPS OF A PR CRISIS COMMUNICATIONS PLAN

A PR crisis plan is a living document. As your startup grows and becomes more complex, having your PR team review and revise this every quarter or so is a good move. Below is a detailed overview of a crisis-communications plan. Like a term sheet, you should know every part of it, if not be moderately familiar with each part, because when a crisis hits, familiarity will ease action.

STEP 1: CENTER YOURSELF

As you know, you're going to have a lot of ups and downs building a venture-backed startup. This is another down, but like everything, it will pass. Get into the mindset of responding versus reacting. Responding is a thoughtful choice, while reacting is usually a rash defense. You've got this.

STEP 2: GATHER FACTS

Many founders want to move immediately and convey some communication when their startup is getting pounded by various stakeholders as a crisis is brewing. Take a pause though. Gather the currently known facts to ensure you have as much information as possible to inform your messaging. You'll want a document that answers:

- What happened? Use bullet points.
- Where did it happen? Online or in the cloud, or is this a physical situation?
- When did it happen, if known? Be as precise as possible.
- When did we know of the situation?
- Who and how many have been impacted to date?
- Is danger imminent?
- Are any authorities, such as police, regulators, medics, and so on, involved?
- Do authorities need to be informed?
- How complete is our knowledge of the situation right now?
- What is the potential impact, to the best of our knowledge?

One note: Knowing all the information in an emerging situation is rare, and the information may change. As a founder, though, you know how to take action with the information you presently have. It's time to construct your plan and move to Step 3.

STEP 3: CREATE YOUR PLAN

With the information you've gathered, you now can assemble your team, tee up your spokespersons, and start your communications to address the situation that's unfolding. There are a lot of parts within this step, so hang in there with me:

1. Pull the crisis comms team together: Even if you don't have an official comms or marketing team or function at your startup, you're going to need to appoint one for the crisis unfolding. You'll need to be involved alongside anyone senior enough to handle a complex and evolving situation. This team shouldn't include seventy-eight people. Consider keeping it to less than ten, though there is no correct number, in order to stay fluid and fast. Communications team members could include:
   A. A board member familiar with crisis communications who is also your ally.
   B. Your co-founder (but you may not want to include multiple if you have them because too many cooks in the kitchen can be problematic).
   C. A member from your C-suite, like your CTO who is a rock under pressure.
   D. Your outside PR agency or freelance publicist if you have one. This is not the time to haggle over a fee, and a good partner will be fair and move exceptionally fast.
   E. A head of sales who works closely with your customers and has insights on the impact of the crisis on them.
   F. A senior comms/marketing person at one of your VC funds. I mention "senior" because now is also not the time to try to work with a person who has been in PR for eighteen months in total. As mentioned, there are, unfortunately, some pretty green platform folks at some VC funds.
2. Suss out stakeholders: With your crisis comms team together,

now take stock of your various stakeholders. These may include customers, investors, your employees, vendors, and the like. Put them all on a list and answer:

A. What is the potential impact of this crisis on this stakeholder? High, medium, or low?

B. What is the best form of communication for this stakeholder? Email, phone, Slack, Zoom, mail, social, in person, other?

C. What is the contact information for *each* stakeholder? (Link or indicate where the contact information exists for each stakeholder. You may have an email address for one, for instance, and then perhaps the LinkedIn profile and cell phone number of another.)

3. Appoint the spokesperson(s): Someone within your crisis comms team should have this role. This may, in fact, not be you as the founder if you're not up to speed with your media training. Rather, this spokesperson or two should have the authority to speak to the crisis and the command to communicate about it well.

4. Write up your holding statement: This is the very first official communication you'll be issuing to your stakeholders, and speed is essential. Get your holding statement out as soon as possible, ideally within a few hours. Otherwise, you'll be stirring the pot of speculation. A holding statement isn't a diatribe or sob story. Instead, it's a proactive communication to your stakeholders that conveys you are well aware of the situation and are taking action. Elements of a holding statement include:

A. An expression of empathy or emotion, if appropriate.

B. The date and time of the situation.

C. Where it happened.

D. Details of the situation that are known and confirmed.

E. When your startup became aware of the situation.

F. Whatever actions your startup is taking that you can disclose right now.

G. Where or how stakeholders can receive updates on the situation.

H. Further contact information, if needed. Here are two examples of holding statements to get you going:

    i. "Earlier this morning, on July 7 at approximately 7:00 a.m. PT, we were made aware of a data breach impacting our customers located in California. Our team is assessing the situation and will provide immediate updates as more information becomes available. The safety of our partners' data is our top priority at (the name of your startup). For any questions, please contact (contact information)."

    ii. "We are currently engaged in a legal matter concerning an issue related to (known information that you can disclose). This matter is evolving, and we are limited in the information we can share at this time. We are working to resolve this matter swiftly and are working with the proper authorities. For any questions, please contact (contact information)."

I. In addition to the holding statement, we like to create an anticipated FAQ document. The FAQ doesn't need to be public, but your spokespersons can have it at the ready in case questions arise. To develop the questions, go wide in your thinking. What absurd or obscure questions could your stakeholders come up with? Write them down and then craft the answers.

5. Create your timeline: Yes, there's more. With your holding statement ready to go, you need to determine where and when it is going to the various stakeholders you defined in 2., above. A holding statement should be issued as quickly as possible,

as mentioned, in the best format for your stakeholders. Your crisis-communications team may want to divide and conquer in this phase, with certain team members taking over the communication with employees while another handles individual phone calls to investors. In addition, your timeframe should include the frequency of messaging. I created something at BAM called "Don't Let Me Ask," or "DLMA," which means don't let your boss/stakeholder/partner/investor even wonder about the status of something. Be so ahead that they don't even get the chance to ask you for an update. This absolutely applies in crisis communications. You may consider hourly or twice-a-day updates, depending on the situation at hand.

6. Create a stakeholder dashboard: This can be as simple as a Slack channel or Google Sheet that tracks incoming communications needing attention. Immediate response is the best policy so you don't fan the flames and cause anyone to wonder further what is going on. If it's not clear already, your schedule should be clear while a PR crisis is unfolding.

STEP 4: ISSUE COMMUNICATIONS

Following your detailed plan above, execute the holding statement to your stakeholders. Then, see how the situation evolves while you collect more information.

Once you know more details, you can move to issuing a full statement. This should only happen after you know the full extent of the situation and when you have a clear plan of how you're moving forward. A full statement is a public apology with commitments behind it, and it may be issued days or even weeks after the PR crisis hits in order to fully flesh out the actions you'll commit to. You'll follow your stakeholder plan outlined in 2., above.

You can dig up countless full statements from nearly every

major company because getting into hot water is inevitable in today's world. A good full statement has the following elements:

- It details what, when, and why the situation occurred.
- It expresses empathy and remorse.
- It has clear actions that your startup is enacting.
- It has a timeframe for updates.

STEP 5: REVIEW AND ASSESS

As the PR crisis unfolds, checking in three times a day, if not more frequently, is not a bad idea. As things simmer down, and they will, a top-of-day and end-of-day touch base is a good call. Post–PR crisis, for days or several weeks, gather the crisis-communications team and conduct a debrief. Here's a list of questions we like to go through with our partners in a Start/Stop/Keep framework:

- Overall, how do we feel we performed on a scale of 1 to 5, with 1 being "extremely poorly" and 5 being "exceptionally"?
- What are the main reasons for this answer?
- If a PR crisis happened again, what would we "keep" in how we handle it?
- If a PR crisis happened again, what would we "stop" in how we handle it?
- If a PR crisis happened again, what would we "start" in how we handle it?

A full crisis plan can be several pages, but here is a simple crisis comms plan example that includes a number of elements covered above. We were super proactive about this plan, even though the likelihood of anything erupting from laidoff folks was low.

\<STARTUP> CRISIS COMMS LAYOFF PLAN
OVERVIEW

\<STARTUP> is conducting a layoff of 10 percent of its staff this week. The team will be informed on Wednesday, 11/6 by 3:00 p.m. ET/noon PT.

\<STARTUP> wants to be prepared in case any media inquiries come through. The quotes drafted below are meant to be used as needed for any inbound requests.

BAM will help monitor media coverage, social media, and Glassdoor reviews and will flag anything relevant.

IMPORTANT TO NOTE

- More often than not, company layoff news for a startup won't get picked up. While it is always a possibility, we advise only considering a response if you receive a direct question or inbound from the media.
- Do not proactively engage with media.
  - Direct all inbound media requests through BAM to vet and recommend how to best proceed.
- Posts on LinkedIn from employees expressing that they were recently laid off and looking for work could also alert the press.

RECOMMENDED MEDIA STRATEGY

BAM recommends evaluating any media inquiries individually:

- If a reporter is asking for an interview about the EV industry at large (slower adoption, interest rates, etc.), we will vet and consider offering \<CEO> for an interview.
- If a reporter wants a story about \<STARTUP>'s layoffs specifically, we provide a quote and nothing else.

Social:

- BAM recommends not posting anything on LinkedIn or other social channels for the time being. If there's any media appetite for a story, we can discuss <CEO> reactively posting a statement to LinkedIn.
- LinkedIn post for Carter:
  - "Yesterday was a challenging day for <STARTUP>. We made the difficult decision to restructure our team to align with our growth priorities across regions. This decision was not made lightly, as I acknowledge this team's efforts have been instrumental in shaping our company and our goal to advance electric vehicle infrastructure and accelerate sustainable transportation. While this step was necessary to position our resources for long-term success, our commitment to our mission remains unwavering."

Glassdoor:

- BAM will support monitoring Glassdoor reviews on Wednesday and flag anything as needed.
- <STARTUP>:
  - Only respond to factual inaccuracies or common themes raised in multiple posts. Do not engage in emotional or defensive exchanges.
  - Responses—if any—should be professional, empathetic, and focused on <STARTUP>'s values.
  - Use the opportunity to highlight <STARTUP>'s commitment to employees, users, and the company's mission, but avoid appearing dismissive of the feedback.
    - General response example: "Hi. We know how difficult these changes have been on the team, and the decision

to reduce our team was a tough one to make. We are grateful for the contributions you made during your time at <STARTUP> and wish you all the best as you move forward. If you would like to share more feedback, please reach out via email to support@_____.com."

MEDIA-FACING QUOTES (TO USE AS NEEDED)
General Company Statement

- **Option 1**
  - "We remain deeply committed to the community we've built. Even in these challenging times, we'll continue to find meaningful, cost-effective ways to come together, collaborate, and celebrate our shared mission. As we close out 2024, we stand at the edge of a transformative period in transportation driven by the accelerating adoption of EVs. Although we've seen recent fluctuations, 2025 is poised to be a pivotal year, with policy, infrastructure advancements, and innovation setting the stage for widespread EV integration. <STARTUP> is prepared to navigate these shifts and lead the way in this vital industry."
- **Option 2**
  - "Today, we made the difficult decision to restructure our team to align with our growth priorities. These decisions were challenging but essential to ensure <STARTUP>'s financial stability as we move toward profitability by 2026. While we're not planning further cuts, we're taking a more measured, data-driven approach to sustainable growth that supports our long-term goals. Our commitment to the <STARTUP> community remains strong, and we will continue to find meaningful ways to connect and collaborate."

SPOKESPERSONS

Name, CEO, phone and email

Name, COO, phone and email

GENERAL DOS AND DON'TS

I'll close out this section with some recommendations on the dos and don'ts of PR crises from what we've observed over the years. Here we go:

Dos:

- If it's emotional, it's probably because people are impacted: No one breaks into tears about a rainstorm. They get upset when the rain is flooding their home. Keep people in mind, and lean in all the way, as best you can, with empathy.
- This isn't the time to blow off preparation: If you're a spokesperson, you need to know every element of the situation that is understood, hands down.
- Rip it off like a Band-Aid: If the news is bad, tell it fully and up front. There is no point in "easing" anyone into the information. Transparency should be your guiding principle in how you run your startup.
- If you don't know, say so: It's okay to say, "I'll have to get back to you on that detail," or, "I'm not sure. I want to provide you with that fact, so let me come back to you."
- It's your fault: I don't even need to hear about what happened to know this truth. You're the CEO, unless you've moved on to just being a board member. The buck stops with you. If it doesn't, get a job working for someone else. As such, convey your responsibility and use the word "I" in taking responsibility.

Don'ts

- Do not be breezy: Do not downplay or bluff anything about the situation. You're not in the boardroom where you may get away with redirecting board members' attention elsewhere.
- Do not name names: I don't care if Bob was the one who imploded your security. Go with grace and resist the urge to throw people under the bus. Remember, it's your fault for hiring Bob in the first place.
- Nothing is off the record: Particularly at this time, you should completely embrace that everything you say, publicly or privately to your internal team, for instance, is up for grabs for the media.

CRISIS SCENARIO PLANNING

You can easily run through the five steps outlined above whenever a PR crisis emerges, and now you know the detail a PR crisis requires. To take it up another notch, consider working with your PR team on crisis-scenario planning. Of course, no one can anticipate *all* the various crises this wild world may hand your venture-backed startup, but here are a few common ones we've seen to spur your imagination:

- Financial fraud: Someone misused funds at your startup, like a CFO buying a boat for a family member or the startup at large misapplying federal funds to deposit money elsewhere.
- Lawsuit: A lawyer friend of mine once told me, "You're not in the big leagues until you get sued." I haven't found a startup yet with more than one hundred employees that hasn't faced a lawsuit, and in the United States, we're just a litigious country. Since lawsuits are becoming increasingly common, add this situation to your scenario planning.

- Supply chain disruption: Did you promise a certain product would be shipped at a certain time? That's often foolhardy as supply chain issues, from tariffs to wars, are an ongoing reality.
- Natural disaster: A hurricane has taken out one of your warehouses or a tornado is going to halt your plans for your entire conference.
- War: I know, but that's the state of our world and a concern as more remote talent around the world is used within one company.
- Security breach: Every Social Security and credit card number of your customers is now floating around on the dark web because you got hacked. Or consider an inside job where a pissed employee releases private information.
- Outage: No one can log into your company's website, and you're powering an entire industry or marketplace.
- Death: Someone in the C-suite dies suddenly, ranging from suicide to a freak accident.
- Viral social media post: An employee films something at the workplace and posts it online, where the internet inhales it.
- Negative press: You botched a media interview, and Sleuthy Sally didn't miss a beat. She published a long and unflattering piece about your startup.
- Scandal: Did an executive sleep with a subordinate and now an investigation is underway? If you employ humans, add this to the list.

I know this isn't the "fun" chapter, but it's real and part of being a Flack Fairy. I have one more topic to throw your way. Then, we'll move on to how professional help can support you and your startup.

EMERGING CRISES THAT AREN'T YOURS DIRECTLY: THE 3W FRAMEWORK

Now that you have a handle on all the crisis moments that could happen to your startup and what to do when they inevitably occur, there's another nagging consideration in the realm of crisis communications: what to say about a crisis that isn't yours.

In the past several years, CEOs and founders have been elevated to "corporate activists."[26] Yep, now you have another job, which is to consider what, if anything, to say about everything else happening in the world. As you know, horrendous things happen in the world around the clock, and you'd be spending every hour of your day responding to every incident, which is unwise, let alone impossible. You can also get into hot water for not saying something though, which seems like an agonizing double-edged sword, and it is.

I created what I call the "3W framework," a rubric to help you weigh your decision of whether to say something or not. The framework is built on three key questions, each with a score ranging from one to five points, with one point meaning "completely irrelevant" and five points meaning "absolutely relevant." Here are the questions and what to consider for each:

WHERE IS IT HAPPENING?

First, consider where the crisis is happening. Is it in the city where your startup is headquartered, clear across the nation, or on the other side of the world? Proximity should earn more points. For example, when Georgia Republicans passed a law that restricted voting access, a flood of companies cried foul, saying it would dis-

---

26 Gerald F. Seib, "Why Business Leaders Are Taking Political Stands," *The Wall Street Journal*, April 19, 2021, https://www.wsj.com/articles/political-systems-failures-compel-corporate-activism-11618842598.

courage voters of color.[27] Delta, which is headquartered in Georgia and is the state's largest employer, issued a muted response but didn't actually rebuke the law. That led to some backlash, including calls for a boycott and protests. The company quickly pivoted, with Delta CEO Ed Bastian saying he wanted to "make it crystal clear that the final bill is unacceptable and does not match Delta's values."[28] Using the 3W framework, Delta likely would have given this situation five points because it happened in its home state.

WHAT ARE YOUR VALUES AND MISSION?

Next, ask how the news aligns with your startup's bigger purpose. Keep in mind that there won't be an obvious link to your mission statement or startup values, as most are sweeping and broad, but take a critical eye to them. Here's an extreme example, but I want to provide one that shows how your values can be tied to an event in a far-reaching way. When the US Capitol was stormed by violent protesters, Disney apparently saw it as an affront to its core values and wasted no time condemning the attack.[29] Disney CEO Bob Chapek called the riots an "egregious and inexcusable assault on...our democracy."[30] He encouraged our society to unite under

---

27 I am going to use real-world examples to help illustrate the framework, which just means I'll have to update the editions of this book more often, but that's okay; Rachel Treisman, "'Based on a Lie'—Georgia Voting Law Faces Wave of Corporate Backlash," NPR, April 1, 2021, https://www.npr.org/2021/04/01/983450176/based-on-a-lie-georgia-voting-law-faces-wave-of-corporate-backlash.

28 David Gelles, "Delta and Coca-Cola Reverse Course on Georgia Voting Law, Stating 'Crystal Clear' Opposition," *The New York Times*, last updated April 5, 2021, https://www.nytimes.com/2021/03/31/business/delta-coca-cola-georgia-voting-law.html.

29 Alexandra Del Rosario, "Disney CEO Bob Chapek Denounces 'Inexcusable Assault' of Violent Attack on U.S. Capitol," Deadline, January 7, 2021, https://deadline.com/2021/01/disney-ceo-bob-chapek-inexcusable-assault-capitol-violence-1234667078/.

30 Lexy Perez, "Disney CEO Bob Chapek Calls Violence at U.S. Capitol a 'Sad and Tragic Day for Our Country,'" *The Hollywood Reporter*, January 7, 2021, https://www.hollywoodreporter.com/news/politics-news/disney-ceo-bob-chapek-calls-violence-at-u-s-capitol-a-sad-and-tragic-day-for-our-country-4113442/.

"our shared values, including decency, kindness, and respect for others."[31] Using the 3W framework, Disney likely would have given this situation four or five points.

WHO ARE YOUR PEOPLE?

Lastly, think about how the news impacts your people. By "people," I mean all your current and potential customers, your employees, your investors, and other stakeholders. Consider how Nike responded to former NFL quarterback Colin Kaepernick, who polarized the nation when he knelt during the national anthem in protest of racial injustice.[32] Nike threw its support behind him, even tapping him for a major ad campaign. Nike CEO Mark Parker said he was "very proud" of that campaign, adding that it helped the company "connect and engage in a way that's relevant and inspiring to the consumers that we're here to serve."[33] Supporting Kaepernick made sense for Nike because the company exists for athletes like him, their millions of fans, and the millions more who aspire to be like them. Using the 3W framework, Nike likely would have given this topic a solid five points. A company that produces cereals and pastry dough, however, probably would give it one to two points, tops.

31   Perez, "Disney CEO."

32   Tom Krasovic, "Colin Kaepernick Takes a Knee During National Anthem in San Diego and Is Booed," *Los Angeles Times,* September 1, 2016, https://www.latimes.com/sports/nfl/la-sp-chargers-kaepernick-20160901-snap-story.html.

33   Lauren Thomas, "Nike CEO Mark Parker Says He's 'Very Proud' of the Kaepernick Ad Campaign," CNBC, September 25, 2018, https://www.cnbc.com/2018/09/25/nike-ceo-mark-parker-says-hes-very-proud-of-kaepernick-ad-campaign.html.

TALLY YOUR SCORE

After you've worked through the questions, add up the score. I suggest running the 3W framework by a handful of your team members to gain an array of perspectives on where a particular issue lands. If the issue earns four or fewer points total, don't take a stand on the issue. If it earns five to nine points, consider issuing a statement. Work with your PR team to strategize your next steps so you don't have to go back to the earlier part of this chapter to do full-blown crisis planning. Even a simple statement on your LinkedIn or internal Slack channels can erupt into crisis. If the issue earns ten or more points, prepare to make a comment and back it with a clear why and, ideally, action or steps. Again, work with your PR pros to craft a timely response. Remember too that *not* saying something can get companies into trouble, though a benefit of being a startup is that you're not a Fortune 500 yet.

This was a scary chapter, but that's not the point of it. This is a complex and ever evolving world we live in, and you have to embrace this as a founder growing an ever-larger venture-backed startup. The good news is there are many forms of communications help, and the next chapter will guide you through how to consider which help may be right for you.

CHAPTER 8 SUMMARY POINTS

- Like insurance or a prenup, crisis comms prep is not fun but is a good idea to have in place, no matter the size of your startup.
- Most events don't explode into a PR crisis, but having your playbook ready as well as being familiar with scenarios that could unfold are good steps to preparing for a PR crisis.

Chapter 9

Hiring the Best Help

———

A common confession we hear from venture-backed startups goes like this: "Well, we've worked with two other PR agencies before, but they just didn't get it." Another version goes: "Well, we tried to hire this freelancer, but after a few months, she just seemed to run out of contacts to pitch and then took this other full-time role." My favorite admission sounds like: "Well, this agency we had represented these big Fortune 500s, but they couldn't seem to be as fast and nimble as us."

So many wrong PR hires tend to be wrong for two reasons. First, publicists are like VCs. Most are decent, some are bad, and a few are exceptional. Unlike lawyers or pilots, there aren't any qualifications or standards for becoming a publicist or VC. A founder could assume that an agency with a lot of clients or a VC with a lot of fund rounds is correlated with excellence, but that's not always the case. Publicists and VCs, much like founders, are often great at selling themselves. They didn't get all those clients and LPs by not knowing how to woo those they wanted.

The second reason venture-backed startups seem to miss on hiring the right PR resource is on them. Most don't know who they need and when they need it. This chapter aims to address the who and when as well as offer guidance on how to hire an agency, if that's the best path. Your aim as a Flack Fairy is not to do *all* the work of a publicist but to be dangerous and dominating enough to be effective, bringing on resources as you need to achieve earned media, win awards and speaking opportunities, and avoid PR crises. Let's start with the various options of who can help with your venture-backed startup's PR, which is often related to the stage of your startup.

DO IT YOURSELF (DIY)...IF AT ALL
IDEAL FOR: PRE-SEED AND SEED

As mentioned, there aren't any requirements for becoming a publicist. This means you can pitch your own stories to the media and try your hand at media relations, as I covered in Chapter 4 about pitching. That's the good news, but the hard news is that you more than likely have nothing of media value at the pre-seed or even seed stage. I've been a mentor at Techstars, one of the largest pre-seed incubators in the US, for various years on and off, and I'm often miffed when a pre-seed founder asks, "So we don't have an MVP out in the market just yet and probably won't for twelve months, but what do you think we can pitch to *The Wall Street Journal* right now?" My answer is consistently, "Nothing." When you're still figuring out what your product offering is, let alone who it is for (otherwise known as your ICP), your focus should be solely on getting your product to market, learning from customers, and making revenue happen. As your investor, I'd be pissed if you were diverting time trying to chat with the media while there wasn't a single paying customer on your books. Of course, there are exceptions at the seed stage, such as if you're a huge name in the tech world with a massive exit or two under your belt. At this stage, you should only approach the media or pursue a DIY approach to announce a seed round, which a number of tech media outlets do cover. Reference Chapter 4 for more on that, but first consider the resources your VCs may have.

YOUR VENTURE CAPITALISTS' PLATFORM TEAM
IDEAL FOR: PRE-SEED, SEED, MAYBE SERIES A+

Several years ago, VCs got a bit savvy and thought to establish "platform" teams to help their portfolio companies grow faster. These platform folks typically support the portfolio companies of the venture fund in several ways, including hiring key talent, creating a brand framework, making introductions to key customers, recommending resources like PR agencies, and more. In fact, there's now a whole international group, VC Platform, made up of thousands of platform folks who gather annually around the world to talk shop about how best to help portfolio startups while balancing conflicting priorities and multiple bosses, often the VC partners who cut the checks to your startup.[34]

Platform teams typically come with your term sheet. That is, there isn't a cost to getting their help on something like a press release or funding announcement. If there is, you need to have a serious conversation with your VC. Make sure to ask your VC what resources are available, and if you're in luck, they may have a dedicated comms and marketing pro who can work closely with you to get a story placed, likely related to a funding announcement, which is in the fund's interest too. Larger funds with more than $1 billion under management often have entire platform teams, while funds under $100 million may only have one dedicated platform

---

34   For full disclosure, I've spoken at VC Platform events a number of times as a sponsor, and VC Platform has also been a sponsor of our annual VC Comms Con.

person. If there is such a platform resource at whatever size VC you get a check from, absolutely ask about how it can help you.

Hold your horses though. The comms and marketing platform folks are not meant to work with you over the course of a whole year, landing you multiple stories related to a product launch, a new big client, a major hire, your latest data report, and so on. A comms and marketing platform pro should be able, schedule permitting, to work with you heavily for a month or two to secure a funding announcement or other notable story. Don't expect more as they have other portfolio companies to help and are often doing seventeen other jobs, rather like you as a founder.

Let's say your VC does indeed have a good comms and marketing platform person available. Make this person your friend because they don't owe you anything and you want something for free. The good ones have a PR process down pat to run you through and will be direct on what is feasible for a story or not. A seed round of $7 million may make it into *Axios*, *Fortune*'s *Term Sheet*, *Business Insider*, VentureBeat, *TechCrunch*, and perhaps some trade publications that are significant to your industry. There's only a very slight chance a bigger publication, like the *Financial Times* or *The Wall Street Journal*, will be interested unless you have a household name as a founder or investor or some other extraordinary aspect of your funding round or startup. That said, good comms and marketing platform folks will have solid media contacts and many media placement examples to show you from other portfolio companies they've helped. It's also absolutely fair to ask who they know and how they'd pitch your funding round to make sure your expectations, as well as theirs, are aligned.

What about a situation where your VCs don't have dedicated comms and marketing platform teams? Or maybe there are comms and marketing platform people, but they're tied up or not really focused on pitching stories for portfolio companies?

These situations are common. A venture fund may be too small to have such a resource, or the comms and marketing platform person or team may be dedicated solely to investor relations or event planning. Frankly, they may also be pretty green and not yet have the chops for landing stories, which is why a candid convo helps.[35] In any case, you can DIY your media relations, as the first section of this chapter mentions, or you could pursue hiring a freelance publicist or agency.

FREELANCE PUBLICISTS
IDEAL FOR: SEED, MAYBE SERIES A+

Freelance publicists serve a great role in the ecosystem of the wild world of PR. They're the "in between" before working with an agency, attempting PR yourself, or leveraging your VC fund's resources. Usually an individual or two, freelance publicists keep a tight book of business, working on a few clients at a time as bandwidth is typically their constraint.

In another way, freelance publicists are "in between" themselves. They often haven't been freelance publicists for decades because, at least in our experience, freelancers get too many clients to handle themselves and have to become an agency with employees to keep up or they get snatched up by a bigger agency or in-house role, like at a venture fund or your startup. I like to think of freelance publicists as exited founders. Most exited founders don't sit around for decades, and most freelance publicists don't bump along with three clients.

Finding a coveted freelance publicist who hasn't yet made the

---

35   I do get emails from comms and marketing platform people asking about how to send a pitch, whom to pitch, or even how a pitch is written. Remember, just having a word like "PR" or "comms" in their title doesn't mean that someone knows what they are doing—at all. This rule applies to anyone who holds a job.

leap to a full-blown agency or an in-house role isn't that challenging these days. So many freelance publicists seem to be in the market in the postpandemic era for a lot of reasons: more flexibility and agency, disdain for "the man," new priorities and purpose in life, and so on. Ask for an introduction from a fellow founder, your VC, or even an agency owner. Like most things in the venture world, referrals are clutch.

As with anything, there are advantages and disadvantages to working with a freelance publicist. The first upside is usually attention: As one of the freelance publicist's few clients, you'll likely get plenty of white-glove service. It's important to understand how much attention you'll get, though, and you can skip down to the "hiring" section below in this chapter to read on. Another advantage may be budget. However, I say this with a strong "may." The budget for good freelance publicists can range from as little as $5,000 a month to upward of $20,000 a month. Most founders seem surprised at this, thinking they'll get a "deal" by going with a freelance publicist but then finding that our budgets at BAM, for instance, start at $15,000 a month, as do budgets at other agencies. The higher rates may reflect another advantage to considering a freelance publicist, which is niche experience. If your startup is super technical, you may prefer a freelance publicist who came from an in-house role in your particular industry.

As for the disadvantages with a freelance publicist, a few aspects should be considered. First, how likely is the freelancer to jump back into a full-time or in-house role? This is an honest question to ask. Take a quick look at the person's LinkedIn to see if there's a history of ping-ponging from consultant or freelancer to in-house or full-time roles. You don't want to get a call from your freelance publicist that goes, "Hey, sorry. I'm accepting a job at fancy fund X starting next month, so we'll have to wrap up your work." Another consideration is the tech stack and resources a freelance publicist may lack. Sharing expensive software for media databases, subscriptions to media outlets, and other tools is a long-known workaround in the publicist space, but you don't want to be on the other side of, "Oh, sorry. I can't get the clip because I don't have a login for WSJ Pro."[36] The last and perhaps most important thing to note is simply the limits of one person. It's not feasible for a freelance publicist to be on a texting basis with four hundred individual journalists, so running out of actual media contacts, those who respond fairly quickly to a pitch via email, text, or in-person meetup, is a reality.

In short, a freelance publicist, if you can snag one, can be a great but limited option for an engagement, especially when a resource at one of your venture funds isn't viable and you don't want to hack media relations yourself over the course of several months. The next level of help to consider is an agency.

PR AGENCIES
IDEAL FOR: SERIES A+

You made it past your seed round, have customers, own data, have hired people, and are growing. Let's start with why an agency could be a good fit at this stage of your startup's game. Like the other options already covered, there are pros and cons.

I'll start with the good stuff, which includes depth, data, and cover-and-move ability. Agencies have the benefit of people who share all kinds of resources, contacts, and techniques among each other. Our Slack channel at BAM, for instance, is constantly pinging with media opportunities across teams as well as summaries

---

36 This is one of the reasons I built OnePitch, a monthly SaaS platform and community for publicists that's less than $100 a month; the other guys charge thousands of dollars a year for multi-year contracts for media databases and monitoring.

of a webinar attended by someone or a media insight just heard at one of the forty or so media events we've just hosted. In addition, a PR agency usually has the tech stacks, media subscriptions, and data needed to operate today, simply because they can afford it. We spend more than $70,000 a year just on the tools we need for keeping up with the media. Another benefit of an agency is a term used by Navy SEALs—cover and move—which we like at BAM. The team working on your PR campaign should have your account covered so if someone is out sick or on PTO, your work doesn't stop. Further, while someone on your PR team is staffing a media interview with you, another is sending a pitch to a reporter, and another is with your CTO in person doing media training. Another benefit, and this is coming from my investor lens, is that you can or should be able to get rid of an agency easily. They don't require severance, reference letters, paperwork related to benefits in whatever state they're operating in, and so on. An agency, like a freelance publicist, is not an employee, and that is a benefit in this context.

You're getting the idea, no doubt, that a PR agency is a lot, though at least not an employee. I put this "a lot" in the category of a potential disadvantage. We have a section in our contracts at BAM, which you have to acknowledge with by initialing, that our communication with you is constant. Usually, we're working with a head of marketing or CMO, who is the one we really bug on Slack, text, emails, calls, Zoom, and more on a daily basis. A good agency will be efficient, especially with your time as the founder, but if you're thinking an agency is a "set it and forget it" kind of outsourced hire for you or your marketing team, it's not, at least for the ones getting it done. Another ding on agencies is the bait and switch: You thought you were getting the most sea-soned and savvy members of the agency on your team, who were indeed on the pitch you were so dazzled by, but then find at your kickoff meeting that three people with hardly two media contacts among them are running your campaign. I'll cover how to avoid this classic case in the hiring section below.

Other disadvantages of an agency can be cost and timeframes. Some agencies only do long-term contracts or start at $30,000 a month. I'll be the first to tell you that these aren't likely PR agencies well-versed in venture-backed startups. Often, these are big agencies with hundreds of employees trying to wedge themselves into the venture-backed startup world, like big venture funds that suddenly want to cut checks for seed-stage startups. They don't want to miss out when you're a unicorn or a public company. But that doesn't mean you should sign a two-year contract with no termination clause or put up with their lack of speed or flexibility. A final drawback to agencies is that they aren't there, inside your startup, like a full-time employee. Let's now turn to hiring "in-house" or full-time comms and PR people at your venture-backed startup.

IN-HOUSE PUBLICISTS
IDEAL FOR: SERIES B+

Now you're cooking with grease, as my chess instructor, Lawrence, likes to say. At this stage of your startup, you've got momentum, some major clients or customers, maybe an office, perhaps a company T-shirt, and a pretty busy cap table. Ankle-biter competitors as well as the dominant dinosaurs you're looking to end are probably aware of you. Moreover, you haven't died. That's an accomplishment in the venture-backed startup world, and your investors are probably inviting you to their annual LP meetings where they parade around a few of their star startup founders, a group that now includes you.

At this point, you likely have someone heading marketing at

your startup, a director or VP, and maybe, though rare, a CMO, if you threw enough equity in. We often see these internal marketing folks hired around the Series A stage, though sometimes, a super technical startup pours all its capital into hiring the engineering and development teams and punts the marketing function to a later stage of funding. Whatever the stage, we tend to like the internal marketing person, assuming they have the competence, kindness, and ability to function as our internal quarterback, communicating between you, the startup, and all the other executives who we can leverage for media opportunities. It's a tough and very short road for us as your agency if this internal marketing person doesn't have the command to get us to the right people, is an asshole, or is incompetent. To be clear: Many other agencies or freelance publicists will put up with a lot to keep a good contract, but you shouldn't as time will be wasted on an inept internal marketing person.

By the time you're considering an internal comms-specific hire or PR specialist, you should have an internal marketing person you absolutely trust. This person should have a lot of say about, if not the final say on, bringing this person on board. Typically, the comms or PR specialist reports to your internal marketing person. One thing to avoid, which unfortunately happens too often, is allowing a brand-new internal marketing head to make a bunch of hires right away. I get it; you just got a heap of fresh capital in the door or maybe need to seize upon the market dominance you have, but this can be dangerous for the same reason you wouldn't allow your CTO who's been with you for two weeks to make hiring decisions without your involvement.

As for the benefits of an internal comms or in-house publicist, there certainly are some. The biggest one is that this person is "on the inside" and should explicitly know every aspect of the startup, every C-suite executive who is media savvy (or not), and every product launch, data report, and big hire. Further, since you get a whole person dedicated to the entire function of comms and PR, pitching media can easily be a daily activity. This person should be able to immediately drop everything and pitch your startup for a newsjacking opportunity, detailed in Chapter 4, if the situation arises.

You know I'm now coming with the downsides, of course. This is the investor in me talking to you, and the fact is that an employee has numerous costs. Like your other employees, this hire comes with workers' comp, health insurance, a 401(k), medical leave, tuition reimbursement, equity, and more and needs to be managed, guided, inspired, pushed, and disciplined if need be. It's also more difficult and more disruptive if you need to fire or lay off this internal comms or in-house publicist, as it is with anyone you have to let go. At this stage of your startup, you've likely done some firings and/or layoffs, but if you can avoid another, do so.

THE WHOLE ARMY: VC PLATFORM PROS, FREELANCE PUBLICISTS, AGENCIES, AND IN-HOUSE HIRES
IDEAL FOR: SERIES C+

I know the previous section may have led you to believe, "Ah, great. I can just bring all this comms stuff in house, give it to my marketing head honcho, and call it a day." But at this later stage of your startup, you're beholden to the Law of Conservation of Complexity, or Tesler's law, meaning any system, including your startup, holds a certain amount of complexity that can't be reduced. So, you won't be surprised to hear that at later-stage startups, your in-house comms hires are often working with PR agencies (yes, sometimes more than one depending on regions and specialities).

You may also see those VCs' platform teams pinging you in your inbox because now you're a big deal for your investors, and they like to look good when you look good in the press. This is simply the sport of venture capital, and if you made friends with these platform teams before you became a unicorn, they'll likely be helpful now more than ever. Embrace the complexity, and ensure you have absolute trust in your marketing head honcho, who, at this point, is likely a CMO you either promoted or recruited for.

A SIX-STEP PROCESS TO HIRING A FREELANCE PUBLICIST OR AGENCY

You're at the sweet spot in your startup where a freelance publicist or PR agency now makes sense. Perhaps you've already gotten a handful of referrals from your fellow founders or VCs and want to have a PR agency in place and signed next week. I appreciate your enthusiasm and conviction, but let's cover a few steps that will ensure you don't make the wrong PR-agency or freelance-publicist hire, which will cost time, pain, and money. In this case, slow is smooth, and smooth is fast.

STEP 1: DEBATE AND DEFINE YOUR GOALS

"Debate" is the key word here. Your co-founder, head of marketing, board, VCs, content manager, and a random advisor all likely have an opinion on how they'd like your startup's brand showcased in the media or what the aim of hiring a PR agency or freelance publicist is. We see this first step missed so often: One co-founder will have one vision on the first call, the CMO will have a different view on the next, and then the head of growth hops in after the pitch and declares the approach is totally off. Use a RACI matrix if that helps align your startup's goals, and determine who the final decision-maker is for selecting the PR agency or freelance publicist.

STEP 2: DETERMINE AND DOCUMENT BUDGET, DATES, AND GOALS

You'll make a great impression on your potential PR agency or freelance publicist by coming to the first meeting with a document outlining your goals, core values, ideal timeframe, competitors, budget range, next anticipated funding round, and other pertinent background information on your startup. I love to see a pitch deck from your latest funding round or a prerecorded product demo video. While detailed requests for proposals are standard practice for public companies, there's no need to issue one. A Google Doc or short slide deck will suffice. Letting the prospective PR agency or freelance publicist know who the decision-makers are, as you determined in Step 1 above with your RACI framework, is immensely helpful as well. As for budgets, expect to spend between $10,000 and $30,000 a month for at least a three-month timeframe, which can then expand to a long-term relationship. Don't make the rookie error of saying, "We don't know what our budget is." That's like showing up to a pitch with a VC and saying you don't know how much you're raising, which reflects poorly on you at worst and makes you seem lazy at best.

One last thing before we move to the next step: "Pay for play" PR folks still seem to operate in our industry. I didn't initially think to include a mention of these oddballs, but I recently heard about a Series B startup talking with such a shop. "Pay for play" means a PR person claims you don't have to pay anything until a media placement is secured. Here's the deal: No legit PR person would ever offer this. PR people aren't like real estate agents or contingent lawyers who only get paid if your house sells or you get a judgment in court. Media outlets that hear of these offers usually shut down the PR people hawking this "pay for play" offer. You don't want to be represented by these outfits.[37]

STEP 3: TAKE THREE TO SIX FIRST CALLS WITH PR AGENCIES OR FREELANCE PUBLICISTS AND LIMIT TO TWO TO THREE FOR PITCHES

Shop around if you have time to do so instead of going off just one good referral. It's best to chat with a few PR agencies or freelance publicists as some won't be available, and great ones will tell you immediately if your startup isn't a fit for their focus or interest industries. On an initial call of thirty minutes, a good PR agency or freelance publicist will ask what your dreams are, what your ultimate goal is (e.g., an exit, IPO, or otherwise), and why now is the time for PR. I've included the usual questions we cover on a first call to give you context for what a well-organized PR agency should bring to the table. After you take initial calls, pass on those that do not impress you or just don't jibe with you and proceed with pitches from those that feel like a natural fit. If the first call feels stiff, disorganized, or dismissive, it's not a fit. Don't kill yourself by listening to several pitches you were already lukewarm on hearing, which can be exhausting and a waste of time for your team and the PR agencies or freelance publicists. Instead, after this first call, you should feel heard and excited to see what the PR agency or freelance publicist comes up with next. These are the people who will be selling you to the media, and if they can't listen or match your energy for what you're building, then it's a no.

---

37 Here's a famous article on the topic, now more than ten years old, from *TechCrunch*: Alexia Tsotsis, "You Can't Put a Price Tag on a TechCrunch Post," *TechCrunch*, November 8, 2012, https://techcrunch.com/2012/11/08/we-are-worth-at-least-3k/.

Bonus move: Check out the Glassdoor reviews of each PR agency. If reviews talk about consistent "burn and churn" or it has a poor rating overall, which sadly, a number of PR agencies suffer from, take this into consideration before moving to the next step, no matter how happy you were with a first call. A common reason venture-backed startups search for a new agency is due to their current PR agency's team turnover or inner turmoil, which drags a campaign down, often at the cost of your retainer.

As for the questions you should ask, make sure on this first call to cover how the PR agency or freelance publicist works (listen for a solid process so you don't have to be a manager for someone else), whether all the PR agency's employees are full time, whether you're talking with a PR agency (many boutique agencies have outsourced contractors), what the average tenure of the team is (which should correlate in a positive or negative direction to what you already researched on Glassdoor), and how key performance indicators (KPIs) and measurements are done. Most importantly, you'll want to get clear evidence on this first call, if not already conveyed beforehand, that this PR agency or freelance publicist has had success with several other startups similar to yours at your stage and in your industry. I cannot emphasize this enough. A venture-backed startup is already running countless experiments, and now is not the time for you to see if some publicist your brother knows who sorta used to do fashion PR can swing it for your startup that's focused on enterprise SaaS. Take bets elsewhere.

Here are several of the questions we cover to assess whether you're a match for our PR agency on our first call before we move to Step 4:

- Tell us about your startup. What are the problems you solve, and who do you solve them for?
- What are your business/company goals?

- Upcoming news—why are you looking for PR now, and how does it solve the business/company goals we just talked about?
- What are your key differentiators?
- Who is your target audience? (Decision-makers, users, and influencers.)
- Tell us about your spokespersons.
- What does success look like to you? Which metrics would be meaningful for us to showcase to you on a quarterly basis?
- What is the most important thing you're looking for in an agency partner? What would be a deal-breaker for this engagement?
- What does your approval process look like?
- When would you be ready to start, and what is your PR/marketing budget?

To keep in for situational purposes:

- What campaigns have you executed so far, and what were the results?
- What hasn't worked for your company so far?
- Are you looking for a dramatic shift from your current campaigns?
- Do you have a current content strategy?
- What content formats do you create or would you like BAM's help creating?
- How does content fit into your company's larger marketing strategy and goals?

To include in other communication moments:

- Who would be our point person at your company?
- Do you have any new data you can share?

- Which customers would we be able to leverage in our campaign?
- What do you think you do well?

STEP 4: MAKE SURE ALL DECISION-MAKERS AND YOUR POTENTIAL PR AND MARKETING TEAM ARE PRESENT FOR PITCHES

As much of a scheduling slog as this step may be, its efficiency is well worth it. Have your decision-makers assembled for the pitch and insist that your potential PR agency's team (the people actually doing the work on your account) is on the pitch as well. This avoids the dreaded bait-and-switch situation where you think you're getting one team, while in fact, after you sign, you get a different, often far-more-junior one. If you're chatting with a free-lance publicist, push to have that person as well as any others on this pitch so you can suss out who else may be added as a contracted resource. This step saves several meetings after the pitch and lets you immediately understand how the team will function and jibe together.

Before the pitch, review the materials your potential PR agency or freelance publicist has sent over. At BAM, we send over the deck or Google Doc with the scope of work twenty-four hours in advance or earlier because we don't "pitch" in the sense of talking at you slide after slide. It's way more efficient for you to see materials beforehand and do a "pre-read" so you can get to your thoughts and questions for the team you may be working with during the pitch. As a CEO myself, I don't want to be presented with something for the first time on a call because I don't like surprises, and I detest wasting time. We can all read slides.

In the pitch, ask how your potential PR agency or freelance publicist deals with feedback, conflict, and not meeting expectations. These things will happen. We don't control or own the media, but neither do you. Listen closely to these answers as a long-term relationship with any PR partner is not likely to be perfect at every moment.

Lastly, in this pitch, if you're feeling the fit, ask for at least three references so you can further vet your final choice. An advanced move is to ask for media references; a great PR agency or freelance publicist will be impressed by this and eagerly tee up the intros. One thing to observe as well: Does this potential PR partner tee up well-thought-out email introductions so you can easily connect with the references? Or are you shown a list of names and emails on a slide? A solid PR agency or freelance publicist is not going to add more to your plate. In tandem, your PR agency shouldn't be bugging you five times a month to ask for a reference check with potential clients they've just had one call with. This is why we don't provide references after the first chat. Think of it like the final phase of an interview process for a full-time hire: You're not asking for references unless it's pretty serious.

One note about "boards": On occasion, we'll hear back from a founder who was over the moon to hire us and then admits, "I didn't get board approval." The only job of your board is to determine if you are the right person to run the startup you both own. If a board member is somehow involved in the decision to bring on a PR team or not, bring that person to the pitch meeting. Otherwise, when I hear this "board approval" excuse, it's a sign of a meek founder and/or one who isn't running the startup. I have the same opinion as an investor.

STEP 5: SWIFTLY SELECT THE PR AGENCY
OR FREELANCE PUBLICIST

It's important to not drag this step out for two reasons. First, the team you met at the pitch may not be available if you take weeks beyond your original timeframe. A good PR agency or freelance publicist will tell you how long the team will be held to keep you accountable. Second, delay is the death of news. If your startup has a tangible news moment, waiting on selecting your agency or punting a start date can hinder the chances of achieving your earned-media goals. Make your selection and also inform any other PR agency or freelance publicist you met with of your decision and why you made it. Don't be like some VCs who ghost founders. It's unbecoming and can land you on an internal list named something like "founders to NOT represent." It's a small industry, as you know.

STEP 6: HAVE PATIENCE

Media momentum takes time. We pass on startups that demand a two-week or one-month "quick turn" for a landslide of media results. Even with a pipeline of solid news moments, gaining share of voice amid competitors is a multimonth to years-long process. A PR strategy is a *strategy*, not three tactics strung together for a random month because you're antsy as a founder and didn't do your job in preparing to bring on a PR agency or freelance publicist.

WHEN A PR AGENCY OR FREELANCE
PUBLICIST PASSES ON *YOU*

There's an assumption that all vendors for venture-backed startups, from legal teams to PR agencies, are desperate to represent any well-funded startup that comes along. Solid PR agencies—those with excellent media relationships, long-standing teams, and great clients—are more discerning about whom they represent, no matter the potential revenue or win they'd get with a venture fund. We are always "buyers" and can walk away. Here's the thing though: A good PR agency may not have the bandwidth or accountability to tell you why they gave your startup the polite pass. I want to outline the top reasons you may be passed on so you don't hear such news.[38]

Mixed messages: Just like gaslighting that leaves you confused, mixed messages that change depending on who is in the room are a clear sign that your startup either doesn't have defined objectives or has warped politics underfoot. We've bowed out of the proposal process when we've sensed massive misalignment as mixed messages will likely continue into the partnership.

Claiming to have no competitors: During our very first call with a potential client, we ask, "Who are your competitors?" An answer that sounds like, "None! We're the only one!" or, "It's just us; there's no one who comes close," are red flags to a good agency. It's just untrue that a company has zero competition, and the media will ask about competitors. In addition, you would have never raised a venture dollar claiming this.

Fear and anxiety about the founder (yes, you): A subtle but important red flag is trepidation about the founder from those who work for them. Pet peeves ("She's running behind, once again!") or annoyances ("He just doesn't get exactly how SEO works!") are somewhat okay. However, statements that indicate a founder puts the fear of God in the people who work for the organization are sure to trickle into our partnership. In addition, what solid PR and marketing agency wants to represent such a founder? Not me.

---

38   To be clear, my team and I will tell you because clear is kind.

Holier-than-thou vibes: If your founder wants to be "President of the World," then it's a pass from us. Lack of humility, the inability to say, "I don't know the answer," and a general air of warped importance are hallmarks of spokespersons who will rarely convert media interviews into favorable or flattering coverage. More damning, these spokespersons do not often receive feedback or coaching well. As an example, we had to terminate one of our clients after the CEO failed to convert any of the ten media interviews we secured. Further, the CEO was dismissive of feedback. Unfortunately, we didn't catch the holier-than-thou vibes in the proposal process.

Trash-talking the previous agency (or anyone for that matter) over and over again: One of our favorite statements at BAM is a quote from Maya Angelou: "When people show you who they are, believe them the first time."[39] A previous PR agency may have botched the work or had a team that changed every sixty days, but unending criticism shows us the feelings aren't resolved, clear and kind communication such as radical candor doesn't exist, and maturity to simply move on with grace and humility is missing. Moreover, we're likely to be the next target if the work or the relationship goes astray.

Burn and churn: The CMO has changed three times in two years. The marketing team has dismissed more than 50 percent of its team in a quarter. Everyone in the C-suite, including the CEO, has been there less than six months. These are classic indications of an unstable startup. Reorganizations, acquisitions, and reductions in force happen. For us, it means an organization may not be strong enough to have PR representation.

---

39 Joan Podrazik, "Oprah's Life Lesson from Maya Angelou: 'When People Show You Who They Are, Believe Them' (VIDEO)," HuffPost, March 14, 2013, https://www.huffpost.com/entry/oprah-life-lesson-maya-angelou_n_2869235.

There's a lot of help out there in the world of public relations. The problem, like anything involving people, is that it's hard to find great help. This chapter should give you some confidence in enhancing your chances of finding the great kind. Just because you found your great team, though, doesn't mean your job is over, Flack Fairy.

CHAPTER 9 SUMMARY POINTS

- There are several "levels" of PR help you can get, including leveraging your VC's platform team and deploying a handful of agencies alongside your internal team.
- Follow a process and ask the right questions to make sure you bring on the PR help that's right for your startup. Too many startups have "bad" experiences due to their lack of PR expertise and just too many subpar PR people out there.

Chapter 10

Partnering with Your PR Team to Drive the Best Outcomes

Now that you have a PR team in place, your goal is to become your team's favorite call of the week. If you're reliable, candid, and a joy to work with, then your PR team is going to be more enthused to deliver results. You already know this as a founder in managing employees, but your comms team is the strongest extension of your brand as their function is to speak on your and your brand's behalf to media and potentially others, such as investors, other employees, regulatory bodies, and more. You want them to be proud and happy to work with you, even honored and moved to do so. That's your goal, Flack Fairy, because then you'll expand the caliber and volume of earned media for your startup thanks to a great team helping you. Below are the top seven tips for becoming your PR team's favorite call of the week.

SEVEN CALL TIPS
SET A PACE

From day one, the cadence and channels of communication, whether you're working with a PR agency, a freelance publicist, or your internal PR team, should be set. Ideally, your team will outline what's needed, but you need to tell them what works for you. This means clearly spelling out how often you expect to be in touch and how you like to be reached. If emails bog you down, just own it. If you live on Slack, keep the daily updates there. If you answer every text the moment you receive it, then establish that as the means to reach you immediately when there's a pressing media opportunity. Revise your communication channels, if needed, on a quarterly basis.

COMMIT TO ACCOUNTABILITY

Once you've stated what your best channels of communication are, stick to them. Chasing you to get an answer is a waste of time, and rescheduling meetings should only be done when absolutely necessary. You're busy putting out fires all the time, and that is well understood, but pushing meetings will drag down your PR team's momentum. Within the first two weeks of working with your PR team, schedule standing quarterly reviews. Confirm who will attend these too. This makes it clear from the onset that both teams are going to be accountable for their work.

One urging: Stay close. You may have a fantastic CMO, if you're lucky enough to be a later-stage founder, but I can't tell you how many CMOs we've seen burn and churn. Commit to at least two calls a month with your PR team if possible.

HELP YOUR PR TEAM EARN BUY-IN

It's not uncommon to have doubters within your startup who question the true value of any PR work. Be honest about that. Tell your PR team who at your company needs to be impressed, such as the CRO, a board member, or the head of growth who can't stand how "fluffy" media placements are.

HOLD NOTHING BACK

Your PR team cannot, and will not, do its best work if it's lacking information. Be transparent and give the agency the full picture. Freelance publicists, in-house comms, and PR agencies work best when you treat them like partners, not vendors. In a sense, I consider us on par with your legal team. We need to know all the skeletons in the closet as we may need to deal with them on your behalf. Keeping information from the PR team can create blind spots, and the media love to find those once you get big enough. Keeping your PR team in the loop lets them stay two steps ahead, which you definitely want.

MAKE NO ASSUMPTIONS

Nobody is a mind reader, and your mind as a venture-backed founder is no doubt a bit ballistic. If there is something you wish your PR team would do (or stop doing), tell them. Don't assume they will figure it out. In that vein, be direct about your expectations —and confirm that you're all on the same page. This is a good rule in general for all your teams, but for some reason, founders seem shy around comms people, perhaps because of the power they hold with the media.

LEARN AS YOU GO

Along the way, you'll likely have some bad ideas. That's especially true if you're new to the marketing and PR world. It's your PR team's job to challenge those ideas and explain why they won't work well and what will instead. Soak in those learning moments. Over time, this will make you a more beloved partner.

Get More by Not Being an Asshole Kindness goes a long way, and as my mom says, "Kindness costs nothing." Your PR team is just like everyone else, and they'll work harder for people they like. Treating them with respect and kindness is the right thing to do, and it costs you nothing. But it will also help drive their performance. Now, I can already hear a few of you. You're thinking, "I *have* to be dogged and demanding to drive people to their best levels!" I agree with this to some extent, and I am one of those dogged, demanding people. But you can compel people to their greatness rather than scare them into submitting to what you think is great. You can be firm, fair, *and* kind.

You'll have the best chance of yielding solid results from your PR team if you do your part to be an excellent partner. Being accountable, being truthful, and keeping assumptions in check are just a few ways to become your PR team's favorite meeting of the week.

WHEN TO MAKE A SWITCH

Some things don't last forever, as you know. Someone you thought was your ace CTO or amazing head of people just doesn't continue to grow with the startup or even you as a founder. The same can happen with your PR agency or freelance publicist. You may not be able to put your finger on it, so here are a few subtle signs of a stall and when you may need to make a switch to a different resource.

YOUR PR AGENCY OR FREELANCE
PUBLICIST SAYS YES TO EVERYTHING

Does your PR team agree, without any question, to everything you ask for? Does it rubber-stamp a yes, even when your request is a bit outlandish? For example, if your PR agency approves a press release for your new junior hire who just joined the human resources team, this might be a sign you're not in a good partnership or receiving any guidance. A good PR partner will know when to push back directly (like we do), protecting you from a PR nightmare or saving you time and headaches. If your PR team doesn't question your logic, it could mean it is more interested in the quick win (making you happy in the moment) than the end game (building up your startup's reputation, exit, or whatnot).

KPIS ARE MIA

If you can't remember the last time you saw a key performance indicator, it's time to ask. What doesn't get measured doesn't get done. Without clear KPIs, things tend to get too comfortable. Your PR team can start to feel more like a marriage with no metrics to hold one another accountable. But this is a business partnership, and you need to be clearly and regularly measuring its performance.

THERE'S NO INNOVATION

When you ask your PR team about the tools, software, and data the team is now using, do you get blank looks? This is a warning you might be working with a PR team that's gone stagnant. If the PR team isn't innovating internally, it's likely it isn't raising the bar for you either. PR agencies that accept the status quo tend to take the same cookie-cutter approach to representing all their clients.

If you want a PR team that will truly push the envelope, look for proof of it in the agency's culture or the individual's commitment to get better.

DIVERSITY LACKS

You already know that many studies have found that diversity can boost creativity. Take a close look at your PR agency's entire team, if you're working with an agency. Importantly, ask yourself if there's diversity at every level, especially among the leadership team. When a PR agency has a diverse team in place, your strategies have more depth and versatility. It also brings greater cultural insights, which could open new doors you're not even privy to yet. It's a good business strategy, not a political agenda.

TOO MUCH TURNOVER

This is the biggest red flag question to ask: Has your PR team changed two or three times in a year? That's troubling for sure, and if that's the case, you should examine the turnover at the entire PR agency. If there is a lot of turnover happening across the board, that could be indicative of a toxic workplace, and stressed, scared people don't produce great, grand results. I say this with a caveat: Proactively changing up your PR team to gain fresh insights is usually a good move. In fact, it shows your agency is aware of creativity becoming stale. So, in this context, I'm talking about people leaving a PR agency at a very high rate rather than the team being changed up after a few years within the same PR agency.

YOU'RE NOT GETTING FEEDBACK

Every interview you do is "Great!" Every byline draft you write up is "Amazing!" This isn't thoughtful or constructive feedback, and we both know you're not the ace here as it relates to PR. Skimping on feedback means your PR team is skimping on time and attention. Ensure your PR team is taking the time to explain how something is great or not and why something works or doesn't. Remember that building a reputation is not simply "handing over the keys." It's very much a collaboration. Good PR partners who want to build a long-term, fruitful relationship will do that by educating you along the way.

YOU'VE GROWN, BUT THEY HAVEN'T

You started out with a crawl-walk-run approach to PR, and at first, it worked great. But now, you've made several internal marketing hires and have the budget and capacity to take your marketing program to the next level. If your PR agency or freelance publicist can't provide the support you need or point you in the direction of a bigger team that can, it might be time to part ways. Outgrowing your PR agency or freelance publicist can be uncomfortable, but it's a growing pain that sometimes arises. In fact, your PR agency or freelance publicist may be totally missing the ball on measurement, the focus of the next chapter.

We're almost done, Flack Fairy. You've learned about messaging, media interviews, media personas, and how to hire a PR team. And now you know how to be your PR team's favorite client. Let's wrap things up by understanding how to measure PR as well as how to incorporate it into your marketing and sales teams' goals.

CHAPTER 10 SUMMARY POINTS

- Be your PR team's favorite call of the week, if not day, in order to get them more excited to tout you to the media.
- Set up the relationship for success with clear communication channels, ways of working, and radical candor.
- Consider changing up your PR help if you spot some indications that the relationship has run its course.

Chapter 11

Measuring What Matters

John Wanamaker, considered one of the pioneers of marketing in the 1800s, is reported to have once said, "One-half the money I spend for advertising is wasted, but I have never been able to decide which half."[40] You could easily switch out "advertising" for "PR," though I hope at this point in the book, you're realizing the complexity of public relations. It's not just responding to a reporter's email or getting a headline you're proud to send around to your investors and employees. Complexity lies in the measurement of public relations, without a doubt. The good news is that public relations can be measured *to a certain extent*, and I'll cover doing so in this brief chapter.

But first, the bad news: Until we can monitor the literal insides of a human brain, we won't fully know what compels a customer,

---

40 Roy L. Smith, "The Salesmanship of Preaching," in *Winona Echoes: Notable Addresses Delivered at the Twenty-Fifth Annual Bible Conference* (Winona Publishing Society, 1919), 333.

potential investor, or talent prospect to be persuaded to act.[41] Did one billboard really catch the customer's attention and immediately prompt a search for your startup's website? Did your talent prospect do an interview with your startup and then search around online and find a bunch of dazzling press clips that pushed the signing of the offer letter? Did that VC you've been hitting up on LinkedIn and at conferences finally respond to your email because your article in *The Wall Street Journal* went live? No one knows. This is why I laugh when I see those after-checkout prompts that ask, "How'd you hear about us?" I click all the buttons.

As research in the marketing and advertising world has long shown, it usually takes seven or more exposures to a brand before a prospect commits to buy or even recalls a brand's name, hence the "Rule of 7."[42] As a fun prompt at talks I give, for example, I'll ask a room of founders, "Can someone tell me the exact moment they knew of Coca-Cola? How about Delta? Nike? Apple?" No hands go up. Then, I'll ask, "But raise your hand if you know Coca-Cola? How about Delta? Nike? Apple?" All the hands go up. "That's branding in a nutshell. Let's get rolling." For now, let's look at what we can measure in public relations.

I mentioned in Chapter 1 that common reasons founders want to ramp up their public relations are varied: Sometimes, it's to attract VCs, potential talent, or eventual acquirers. Other times, it's to help with top-of-funnel leads or to signal to industry partners that you are legit and active in the marketplace. These are good goals for why you'd like your startup to get ramping on public relations, but the measurements or KPIs need to be set alongside these goals as much as possible. Here are a few we use:

---

41 I know some of you are working on this, but until then, I'll hold off on updating this edition.

42 Check out the Rule of 7 in more detail: "Marketing Rule of Seven," University of Maryland (Baltimore), Communications and Public Affairs, accessed September 1, 2024, https://www.umaryland.edu/cpa/rule-of-seven/.

- Number of media placements: This is basic and can be further refined to the quality of media placements, such as with large outlets that have DAs over sixty or trade media outlets that have DAs over fifty. Be mindful of putting in a quality constraint though. Media relations is a volume game to some extent, as I'll get to when I discuss share of voice, and unless you're a notable late-stage startup, you're better off collecting as many earned-media placements as possible, from trade media outlets to top-tier media outlets. I'm not saying you should do a podcast that your CTO's brother hosts about croissants. You should still have some discernment, but what unnerves me is hearing a founder who only wants coverage in *The New York Times* or *The Wall Street Journal* when the startup is pre-seed stage with a no-name founder.
- Share of voice: This is the most significant measurement we take. Let's say you have four dominant competitors, and compared to those four, you only have a "share of voice," as measured by online presence and links, of 10 percent. Your PR campaign can have a goal of increasing your share of voice to 20 percent over, say, twelve months. The tricky part of share of voice is your competitors and how aggressive they are with their media relations campaigns. If your competitor is Microsoft, for instance, a share of voice comparison may be a fool's errand. Instead, select competitors more at your stage or size, and update your share of voice competitors every six months as your industry evolves and new competitors come into the space.
- Number of backlinks: Backlinks are still important and help your website rank all over the internet. Sadly, we can't control whether a backlink is included in a media piece, and some media outlets refuse to use them. I caution any founder who is solely interested in securing backlinks. That said, getting good links from credible media outlets absolutely impacts your DA

score, as discussed above in the number of media placements. When your DA increases, the ranking of your website increases relative to your competition.

- Lead generation: Another tricky one. While we want to work closely with sales teams, it's hard to be a stickler about counting leads as a sole measurement of media relations outcomes. You could put a form up that asks, "How'd you hear about us?" on your website, but those are subject to lies and people like me who click all the buttons.

- Social media following or website traffic: I like to tell founders, "We get your leads to your door; you take them from the door." Social media following or website traffic is okay to measure, but if not tied to top-of-funnel leads, it doesn't mean much. Traffic that isn't captured and put into your funnel in some way doesn't do anything. Plus, it's easy to manipulate web traffic or social followers. Anytime you see a brand with eight hundred thousand followers on Instagram or TikTok, check out the comments section. Are there two comments left on the latest post? That's a pretty good sign the followers are fake, bought, or bots.

- Ad hoc: This one really drives founders crazy, and I get it. It's hard to measure how many people came up to your booth at a conference and gushed, "Oh yeah! I saw you guys in that great article!" In truth, though, capturing these comments is important. So many of our founders have reported that a great article in a publication led to an inbound lead that was a multimillion-dollar sale. It does happen.

I didn't include "media impressions" in the above list. I couldn't tell you why the PR industry holds on to "media impressions," but it's likely because media outlets still showcase them in their media kits. A media report with 4,380,330,275 media impressions from a month of decent press coverage doesn't mean crap. Run for the hills if you see a PR agency or freelance publicist touting this metric as the best one out there.

Toolwise, there's a slew of software in the PR industry that helps with all the above measurements. Your PR team or freelance publicist should be well familiar with platforms such as Cision, Muck Rack, Agility, Sprout Social, OnePitch, and Talkwalker.[43] You don't need to worry about what software they're using, but make sure you cover how measurement is done, as I discussed in Chapter 9. To give you a clear example of what reporting can include, here are a few slides from a quarterly review we completed for a startup:

BAM

_____

PR
CAMPAIGN
HIGHLIGHTS

- **In (date), BAM secured sixteen media placements,** exceeding KPIs by 60 percent.

- **Positioned (founder) as an AI expert and thought leader** through targeted industry outreach, proactive and reactive pitching resulting in such coverage and/or opportunities in *PYMNTs, Gizmodo, Spiceworks,* and more.

- **Positioned (CTO) as business/overall thought leader in the space** through targeted outreach to consumer, trade, podcast, and broadcast outlets resulting in coverage and/or opportunities in *Sports Business Journal, RFID Journal, Chain Store Age,* and more.

- **Successfully coordinated PR around (brand) opening** including drafting the press release and coordinating outreach, resulting in six BAM-secured placements increasing (startup's) credibility and brand awareness within the retail and sports tech industries.

- **Researched, drafted, and submitted 10-plus award and speaking opportunities**, acting as (startup's) liaison between organizers and (startup) and securing feedback on applications plus information on sponsored opportunities, for organizations like X, Y, and more.

---

43 I am a co-founder of OnePitch, which helps publicists find the best media contacts for their pitches—just full disclosure again.

Insights

(STARTUP) ARTICLES (DATE)

- We saw **69 pieces** of coverage (both by BAM and organic) in the last six months.
- Between Q1 and Q2 we saw a **12.8% increase in potential audience reached**.
- (startup's) coverage spike in the month of April was around the **X and Y announcement.**
- May and June's coverage focused on **our collaboration with (brand)** and inclusion in multiple **retail tech/autonomous tech roundups.**

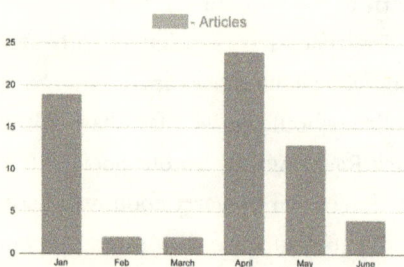

Share of Voice

- **(Startup) earned #2 in SOV** between January and June, at **19.4%** for H1 overall.
  - (Startup) SOV in **Q1** was at **15.1%** and in **Q2** was **29%**, showing a **13.9% increase**.

- (Competitor) stayed at #1 in Q1 and Q2, largely due to its partnership announcement with (brand) in April and XX.

- In Q2, (competitors) trailed behind with **20%, 11.7%, and 8.3%** respectively. (Competitor) saw a decrease in SOV of 15.7% after a spike in coverage in March for the release of its vision analytics platform.

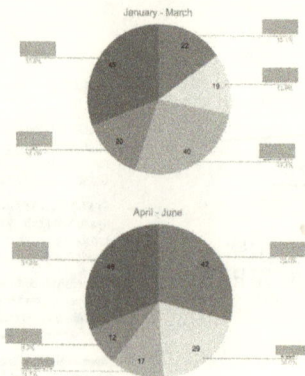

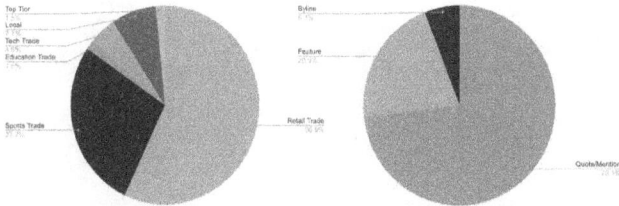

BAM

(DATE): TYPE OF OUTLET & TYPE OF COVERAGE

Top Tier
Local
Tech Trade
Education Trade

Sports Trade

Byline
Feature

Retail Trade

Quote/Mention

Goal for H2 2024: BAM to secure three top-tier mentions and/or features, and coverage across at least three different industry verticals (tech, sports, logistics, etc.)

Now let's get into how your PR campaigns and media placements can be used in tandem with your sales and marketing teams.

CHAPTER 11 SUMMARY POINTS

- Since we don't fully understand how a human brain makes a decision about anything, it's a fool's errand to believe you can fully measure the impact of a media placement, as frustrating as that is.
- Media placements, share of voice, number of backlinks, lead generation, social media following, and ad hoc feedback are a few ways to measure PR.

Chapter 12

Making a Media Flywheel to Enable Sales

If you've made it to this chapter, excellent. You understand what PR is, what pitches to the media look like, who the media are, how to hire a PR team, what to measure, and more. We're almost done, Flack Fairy. This chapter is a short one but perhaps the most important, and that's because venture-backed founders so often fail to link their PR efforts to their sales and marketing ones. Just ahead of writing this chapter, I was chatting with a founder and the startup's marketing lead. The marketing guy said they just couldn't move forward with anything on the PR front because the sales folks weren't "doing their jobs." On the call, I pulled up this startup's website and said, "Well, I see there are no case studies, no testimonials, and no posts on LinkedIn for over five months. The blog hasn't been updated for eighteen months, and the last time the 'news' page had something new was ten months ago. I signed up for your newsletter about three months ago and haven't received anything. Perhaps I missed them. Still, I have to ask: Is it sales' fault?" There was a good eight seconds of silence.

The list of things I rattled off usually falls under marketing, not sales, of course.

The bottom line of this chapter is that if you're now investing in earned media, which you likely are if your startup is gaining traction and you understand the power of PR, you've gotta squeeze the utter life out of it. When you secure earned media, nab an award, or get to speak on a stage, make completely sure your sales and marketing teams are leveraging those wins. I've used this analogy with some founders who speak better in "money": Your shoes are untied because you've been running nonstop. I put one hundred dollars on a table, separating sixty dollars from forty. I tell you to keep running and offer, "You can take the full hundred dollars, but you'll have to tie your shoes first. Or just take the sixty dollars and continue to run." What are you going to do? Most founders will take five seconds, tie their shoes, and pocket the hundred dollars. This is a founder who ensures public relations, marketing, and sales are humming together. The other founder takes the sixty bucks and keeps tripping.

So take all the money off the table. Spend a few moments to ensure your sales and marketing people are in sync with PR and doing everything they can to make earned media work with owned media, as we covered in Chapter 1. Here's a fundamental checklist for the sales and marketing teams to leverage when you get a PR win, award, or speaking opportunity, which we use for the startups we represent as well. In fact, we have an "amplify" team at BAM, rather like a mini marketing arm, that executes a lot of the following. If you're not doing this in house, you can surely outsource it:

- Press page: If you don't have a news or press page, then add one. When you win a media placement, put it immediately up on this press page. Better yet, make sure you signal to the media and anyone else visiting this section of your website that you have your act together and want to get media inquiries. Make sure you have an easy-to-find press email on this page, such as "press@yourstartup.com."

- Social media pages: Ideally, get your media placement, award, or fabulous speaking remarks up on all your social media channels within hours. Tag the appropriate media outlet, reporter, moderator, and so on, if allowed. If in doubt, ask. For example, if you're speaking at a "closed doors" session at a venture fund in some backwoods country estate, perhaps the fund explicitly has a "no social media" policy.

- Venture capitalists: Your VC is likely just as thrilled as your mom is to showcase your wins. You looking great makes your VC look great. Immediately upon snagging a great media placement or award, let your VCs know, ideally through the marketing or comms person on the platform team, if there is one. I can't tell you how many times I've heard someone in the VC comms and marketing community I run say, "I had no idea they were announcing X today!" Now, that poor VC comms and marketing person is in a scramble, so if you know ahead of time that a big win, such as a major award or a media placement in a top-tier outlet, is going to drop, give that person a heads up. Messaging can be as simple as, "Hey, Kerry, we're expecting an article in *The Wall Street Journal* to land any day now. I don't know the exact timing, but I wanted to give you the heads up so you can help us amplify the piece, if it's positive, of course." Bonus: Give your VCs suggested social media posts they can cut and paste if there isn't a platform person at the ready.

- Your team: Besides your mom and your VCs, another group that is usually ecstatic to cheer on a PR win for your startup is the group working in the startup: your team. Now, not every team member of yours is a social media butterfly, but some likely are. Tee up your team with a Slack message or email that includes your own post so they can easily share and comment further.

- Leads and prospective clients: FOMO is a human phenomenon. VCs suffer it frequently because they don't want to miss out on the next unicorn. But your leads and prospective clients also don't want to miss out when it means they'll fall behind, not achieve their revenue goals, or get eaten by competitors. Send your wins to your leads and prospective clients. Your sales folks can determine the best format, whether it be a simple text that says, "Hey, Matt—happy to share this clip of our CEO in Bloomberg today that explains X about the progression of our industry. Looking forward to seeing you next week..." or a more formal email that showcases the win with context on what it provides. The nuance here is to not be obnoxious with a "Look at us!" tone. Rather, tie in WIIFM. Does the fireside chat you did at a *The Wall Street Journal* event drop some juicy intel about where the market is heading? Does that great article in *Fortune* detail some data you haven't shown any players in your space yet? Good. If your lead or prospective client can benefit in some way from your media flex AND be impressed with it at the same time, then you're adding value. Speaking of which, VCs you want to have on your cap table should be considered leads as well. Several startups we've worked with, as I mentioned in Chapter 1, have brought on BAM just to play a hard FOMO game six to twelve months ahead of or during a raise. Use FOMO to your full advantage.
- Influencers: You likely have industry "influencers," perhaps board members, nonprofits, regulatory groups, academics, or experts in your field or otherwise, who have weight in your space. Don't leave these people out. They may not be as elated

to see your media win as your VC or employees, but showcasing your win and having a natural good touchpoint will not hurt.

- Sales, pitch, and press kit materials: You're not done yet. You've now told everyone about your latest media placement or award win within forty-eight hours, which is solid, but don't leave money on the table by not refreshing your sales, pitch, marketing, or any other materials like press kits that usually include media clips, photos, and quotes. You don't have to do so immediately, of course, but once a month is a good cadence to ensure you have the latest wins across all your materials. Make a list of such materials that need updating to keep things seamless.

Like many things discussed in this book, this list isn't for you, the founder, to do yourself. I simply want you to know what needs to be done so you have a handle on whether someone is doing it well or not at all. Don't let a marketing director or lead of yours ever say that things are just too busy to get to the above list if you're engaging with a PR effort. You have a few options: have your PR team take over the list above, whether they are in-house or external, or figure out why you're getting such an excuse from this marketing person. Additionally, you can fire the marketing director, which we see often enough.

CHAPTER 12 SUMMARY POINTS

- Don't let your earned media flame out: There's a lot to leverage immediately with every earned media placement you secure.
- Your press page, social media, VCs, your team, leads and prospective clients, influencers, and all your sales and marketing materials can help amplify your earned media.

Chapter 13

Go Forth, Flack Fairy

——

You're here. We made it. And yet—you know this is just the beginning. I like to ask people, "How are you in five words?" rather than, "How are you?" because the latter usually elicits a quip like, "Good!" or, "I'm fine." Five words can be contrasting, messy, collywobble-y. As a venture-backed startup founder, you'd probably give me a different set of five words every day, if not every hour, if I asked, and that makes total sense. Whatever your feeling is right now, having made it to this chapter, I do hope you're feeling a few particular ways.

First, dangerous. I spilled all the beans I've got, so you now have a grasp of what public relations actually is and could look like for your venture-backed startup. I hope you can flip to a chapter in this book at any time and blame me when you show your CMO or board member, "Well, see. We didn't ask the right questions at all when we hired that PR agency you insisted on." I'm not saying you should do that, but now, you know a hell of a lot more when it comes to what works and what doesn't work in the realm of public relations, and no one is going to play you for the fool.

Second, relieved. Maybe you felt bad that your seed startup

hasn't had a single media mention since you started two years ago, but now, you know you shouldn't even be talking to the media right now. Or maybe you're a Series D founder who is on your third CMO hire wondering why the first two were such bombs, and this book just gave you some answers. There is nothing like the feeling of relief after seeing some light, and I hope this book gave you some.

Third, fired up. You used to want to bang your head against the wall when you saw your competitor get on another stage or in another media outlet, wondering how this was even happening, but now, you know they're simply executing a PR strategy pretty well. You can too. That is powerful.

Fourth, I'm going with "mad." You're a little mad that things as "silly" as messaging, media coverage, and awards actually do something. I get it. One of my favorite quotes from the Greek journalist Nikos Kazantzakis goes, "Since we cannot change reality, let us change the eyes which see reality."[44] That's PR in a nutshell. PR is not changing reality or facts. PR is a microscope, pair of glasses, or telescope, depending on the strategy. You, the founder, get to decide which of those tools eyes will look through.

Lastly, dominating. You're a Flack Fairy now. You know some things. I remember taking my first helicopter lesson years ago, getting the lowdown on aerodynamics and things like Bernoulli's principle and effective translational lift. "Wow," I thought. "So this is how this chunk of metal hovers in the sky." I felt like I was in the club, the club that knew about this special kind of magic most people had no idea about. I hope you feel that now too. You're in the club, and it is called "Club Flack Fairy." You are invisible but a force, undefined but undeniable. And yet you get that a Flack Fairy requires "doing the work." Those headlines, those stage

---

44 Nikos Kazantzakis, *Report to Greco*, trans. P. A. Bien (Simon and Schuster, 1965), 45.

appearances, those snappy phrases don't happen by luck alone. Luck is part of being a killer Flack Fairy, like getting your startup to become a unicorn, but consistent, dogged work is the only way you'll get to this magical, dominating status.

See you on the front page. I can't wait.

Appendix

Sample Scope of Work

A PROPOSAL TO SUPPORT CREATOR COMMUNITY BUILDING, EVENTS, AND MEDIA RELATIONS FOR STARTUP X

Prepared by
BAM
Prepared for
STARTUP X

WHY NOW AND WHY BAM

STARTUP X has created a core platform that enables "high code" markets (organizations with developers) to build their own electronic medical records. The team is looking to build on this success and expand awareness around the benefits of its platform by bringing it to "low code" markets, a much larger audience that currently lacks software development capabilities. STARTUP X is eager to deploy a media relations and community building campaign that engages with STARTUP X Creators and provides the tactical expertise, marketing support, and ongoing insight to drive growth for both STARTUP X and its submarkets. As a result, doctors, nurses, and physicians—regardless of their level of coding expertise—will rely on STARTUP X as *the* go-to resource to help them learn how to customize and innovate software to meet the needs of their patients as healthcare technology progresses.

Below is a snapshot of BAM's strategy to tell STARTUP X and its Creators' unique stories and message to the right audience at the right time. We take a bespoke approach with each client, leading to media relations campaign success that mirrors your business goals. See for yourself; we spell out why BAM is a fit for STARTUP X.

Our dedicated Health Tech Practice (HTP) has worked with a wide range of partners and knows multiple key audiences are critical to the success of our campaign. We get in front of and speak to patients, payers, health systems, and more. Our HTP leverages its relationships with health media, event organizers, analysts, and VCs to increase awareness and credibility and, most importantly, tell your story.

Take a look here at some of our best 2023 health tech coverage wins. Below, you can see additional client websites and coverage tracker samples:

- (Startup)'s data platform fuels healthcare enterprises with actionable provider information, including insurance coverage, prices, and performance. In addition to our media campaign, BAM secured award wins for Crain's New York 100 Best Places to Work, *Business Insider*'s 30 Under 40, and Fierce Healthcare's Fierce 15.
- (Startup) is a software company developing an artificial intelligence (AI) copilot for physicians to help accurately diagnose medical conditions. BAM secured twenty-seven pieces of cov-

erage (64 percent of which were company features) within three months of kicking off the campaign and announcing (Startup)'s Series A.

- (Startup) is a healthcare technology company that works with providers, researchers, and health-focused enterprises in their pursuit of precision healthcare for better patient outcomes. In addition to media, we executed influencer campaigns, top-tier event wins (e.g., SXSW), and media dinners.

- (Startup) provides comprehensive and trusted medical care in the comfort of home to people with serious health concerns. We partnered with (Startup) from their Series B all the way to unicorn status.

- (Startup) creates accessible healthcare using evidence-based design and tech to create the optimal patient experience. The BAM team secured over one hundred pieces of coverage for (Startup) in top-tier outlets like *The Wall Street Journal* and *Fast Company* and coveted trades, including *Healthcare Dive* and *Becker's Hospital Review*.

- (Startup) connects underserved communities to high-quality care by partnering with local health centers and community-based organizations. Following a successful Series A announcement, (name), co-founder and Chief Health Equity and People Officer, had this to say:

  ○ *"BAM, as an agency, also does a lot of great things with events— I've attended 'Media Matchmaking' events they've hosted where they set up speed-dating with various journalists. This helped me be on the radar of specific journalists at Forbes, TechCrunch, and Crunchbase, and they reached out to me for Silicon Valley Bank coverage. The team is an absolute PLEASURE to work with—it feels like they're part of our team, not an external firm. I can't recommend them enough."*

HERE'S WHAT WE'RE GOING TO DO—CARE APPROACH

BAM is a communications agency that believes stories move the world. We move stories forward for venture-backed startups and venture funds that challenge, change, and create entire industries.

Compelling venture-backed startups and venture funds partner with us for our unbeatable strategy of CARE (Connect, Amplify, Reach, and Engage). The data is clear: Our CARE strategy has helped our clients raise 94 percent more than the average venture-backed startup and more than $13.5 billion in total venture funding.

CONNECT

Connect is about expanding your brand's presence. We focus on amplifying your community's voice through a mix of earned media coverage, which includes articles, features, podcasts, mentions, and broadcast segments. Based on our conversations so far, we believe the following will have an immense impact on STARTUP X's brand and community.

PR and Media Relations

We'll build validation for STARTUP X through strong media placements to bolster credibility and trust. We'll lead the strategy and execution of PR, media relations, and thought leadership for STARTUP X and its Creators, which includes managing press inquiries, providing cover for internal and external communication, and performing additional tasks as needed to support comms needs.

- Press release development and execution
- Announcement-driven media relations

- Trend/newsjacking for thought leadership media opportunities
- Proactive angle strategy and pitching
- Internal communication, including investor and stakeholder updates
- Weekly news scans to identify and strategize around industry trends, competitor coverage, and breaking news

Our goal is to secure media coverage and thought leadership throughout target media outlets that reach our key audiences (clinicians, doctors, physicians, nurses) and potential STARTUP X investors and talent. We'll position STARTUP X and its Creators in front of mainstream and business media, as well as health tech, AI, and other trade outlets.

Sample headlines include:

- **"Case Study: How [Health System/Creator] Reduced Physician Screen Time by Y% with a Customized EMR"**—A case study featured in *MobiHealthNews* by (reporter name) highlighting STARTUP X's impact with relevant data. We'll leverage a Creator to discuss why this EMR is specifically impactful within a specified subgroup (i.e., nephrology).
- **"EMRs Have Frustrated Clinicians for Decades. Meet the Physicians Who Are Building Their Own"**—A roundup story with (reporter name) at *The Wall Street Journal* leveraging identified Creators of different specialties to discuss physician autonomy in EMR design.
- **"The Latest Trend in Digital Healthcare: COMMUNITY Xs Who Code"**—A trend piece with (reporter name) at *Modern Healthcare* highlighting (spokesperson)'s thought leadership and referencing the creation of the STARTUP X community and the new wave of doctors interested in the technology that

fuels their practices. In addition to (spokesperson), offer interviews with Creators who can speak to the immediate impact of low-code EMRs on their specialties.

- **"Taking Personalization to the Next Level—How STARTUP X Brought a 'Shopify' Approach to Medical Records"**—A feature story highlighting STARTUP X's unique approach covered in *Fierce Healthcare* by (reporter name).

- **"Long Doctor Wait Times Still Plague the Healthcare Industry. Experts Explain Why Things Haven't Changed and the Tech Aiming to Help"**—Leverage identified Creators for a consumer-focused roundup written by (reporter name) in *USA Today* that explores physician issues and technologies aiming to improve the industry as a sample use case of STARTUP X's EMR platform.

- **"Existing EMRs Don't Work Well for Fertility Clinics. This Physician Is Pioneering a Solution"**—A case study feature story with (reporter name) at *Femtech Insider* highlighting a female Creator within fertility medicine who can speak to how STARTUP X has evolved its practice.

Click **HERE** to review a few of our well-established media contacts in the health tech, business, AI, and VC industries that we have already selected for our media list for STARTUP X. Please note, we'll create a detailed media list on Google Sheets once you become a client.

AMPLIFY

Amplification is key to what we do. It's not just about securing media placements for STARTUP X and its Creators; it's about making those placements echo across your entire network. Our goal is to ensure your target audiences, ranging from potential customers to investors, see STARTUP X consistently on social and owned platforms as much as in earned media.

Content and Marketing Support

Content: BAM will collaborate with STARTUP X to identify content that will help amplify its story. Formats can include thought leadership stories and bylines that amplify STARTUP X's narrative or blog content that aligns with a major news moment or announcement.

Messaging: BAM will draft messaging framework(s) for STARTUP X and its Creators, assisting in the development of and positioning design for website landing pages.

Playbooks: BAM will work with STARTUP X to develop a playbook template that can be used to convey valuable insight and advice, as well as a step-by-step process to help Creators market their custom-built EMRs.

Social: BAM will actively promote STARTUP X's media placements on social media platforms such as LinkedIn, drawing attention to the company's social pages to boost its digital presence and engagement with its targeted audience.

Monitoring: BAM will actively listen, track, and gather relevant content related to STARTUP X's brand, industry conversations, and competitors on social media. Beyond sharing insights, this weekly report will provide detailed action items for STARTUP X to respond to, engage with, or gain inspiration from the content.

Events: When attending or speaking at a conference or event, it's important to strategically leverage your owned channels to create awareness and buzz, share your wisdom, and recap the experience. BAM's marketing team specializes in these moments and will help STARTUP X strategize how to put its best foot forward and ensure STARTUP X maximizes its presence at every event.

REACH

The essence of what we do is rooted in the power of reach. It's all about the magic that happens when people come together face to face. We're not just talking about meetings but about carefully curated moments to spark the most dynamic interactions. As our client, you'll have priority access to our forty-plus invite-only events a year. A few events we feel would be a particularly great fit for STARTUP X include:

- Industry Media Dinners: Intimate invite-only dinners with industry-specific journalists and founders. We have our upcoming summer media dinner series and think you'd be perfect for our health tech dinners below!
  - San Francisco: Tuesday, July 30—Health Tech
  - New York City: Thursday, August 15—Health Tech
- Media Matchmaking Day: Our high-energy "speed dating" event series in SF and NYC brings dozens of top-tier media together to meet you.

Beyond BAM-hosted events, we'll also work with STARTUP X to craft bespoke events for your high-value community and provide ongoing strategic advice around how to "land the plane" and get tangible business ROI from these events. Sample events include:

- Bimonthly Community X Dinner: A bimonthly event hosted in various markets that house larger portions of the community for eighteen to twenty members to connect, talk through challenges, and share solutions and best practices, hosted by STARTUP X. With the STARTUP X team driving the conversation and providing in-person support, BAM will help outline a follow-up process to get attending members into your pipeline.
- Quarterly Community X Workshop: A quarterly event for

thirty to fifty members of the community to gather with a series of meaty "playbooks," prepared by four to five members themselves, which are presented and discussed by the group. STARTUP X will host the event and have members on site to foster relationships and gather contact info, with support from BAM.

- Monthly Webinar Series for Community X: A monthly series of webinars that highlight case studies and playbooks from Community X members themselves on how they've solved prominent challenges. This event will be hosted by STARTUP X and feature a panel of two to three clinicians who will participate in a group discussion for thirty minutes and then open up to Qs and As in the final fifteen minutes.

ENGAGE

Engagement involves direct intros to venture capitalists from our community of 430-plus funds that is managed daily by our CEO, Beck Bamberger. This community meets annually at our VC Comms Con, the invite-only gathering of 120-plus communication professionals from venture funds across the globe.

All venture-backed startup founders are in a state of ABR (Always Be Raising). Our Engage process includes a custom list of target funds and direct email intros to these funds once they opt in for an introduction to STARTUP X.

This Is Some of the Fabulous Team
(Name), Managing Director, People Tech

- *(Name) has been with BAM for ten-plus years and runs the People Tech practice, which houses tech startups that impact the way we work and live. She's worked with a wide range of B2B and B2C startups from early stage to post-exit and is passionate about helping to tell impactful stories that make a real impact on each company's bottom line.*

(Name), Senior Account Manager, Health Tech Practice

- *(Name) has supported clients in BAM's health tech practice for nearly four years. She is focused on developing and executing creative media relations and executive thought leadership strategies across B2B, B2C, and B2B2C clients. She has most recently worked on several companies to help establish and amplify their brand awareness and credibility.*

(Name), Account Manager

- *(Name) is an account manager at BAM on the health tech practice and has been at the company since she was an intern. She leads the team in PR strategy, client communications, account management, campaign development, and media relations. (Name) is passionate about her role in the health tech practice and enjoys working with founders who prioritize improving healthcare access for all patients.*

(Name), Senior Account Executive

- *(Name) is a senior account executive at BAM. She handles media relations, content development, and creative ideation for clients while maintaining day-to-day client communication. (Name) has experience with various clients across the technology industry, including B2B and B2C tech, AI, and other areas.*

HERE'S WHAT WE'RE GOING TO ACHIEVE IN SIX MONTHS

These are our KPIs and what you can expect from us in our partnership together.

OPTION A: FULL-SERVICE CARE
STRATEGY, $25,000 PER MONTH
Media Relations, Media Messaging, Marketing,
In-Person Events, VC Relations
Connect | PR and Media team

- Custom onboarding for goal, audience, and KPI alignment
- Quarterly comprehensive PR plan and tactical timeline
- Quarterly one-hour messaging review to sharpen STARTUP X's why, how, and what and hone competitive differentiation
- Two to three press releases over six months (e.g., launch announcement, Creator/EMR announcements)
- At least ten to twelve media placements in national, business, tech, health tech, and relevant trade outlets
- Monthly proactive angle generation, including angles supporting EMR launches
- Monthly announcement coordination
- Ongoing newsjacking
- Ongoing reactive pitching
- Media preparedness (interview memos, interview prep)
- One news scan per week with up to four competitors
- Weekly meetings for real-time reporting and brainstorming
- Quarterly BAM Insights Reporting

Amplify | Marketing team

- Quarterly strategy session to define priorities and actions, which may include a mix of the deliverables listed below, in coordination with STARTUP X's in-house team that is currently creating and launching small content pieces over the next year.
  - Monthly ghostwritten byline (placed by the PR team) or owned blog content
  - Drafted social media content for LinkedIn to amplify media wins (within twenty-four hours of publishing)
  - Drafted messaging and positioning for STARTUP X's EMR landing pages
  - Drafted PR and marketing playbook for Creators
  - Weekly social scans to flag industry conversations and engagement recommendations
  - Documented social media strategy and marketing recommendations for amplifying STARTUP X's presence at industry events, conferences, and speaking opportunities
  - Press page updates, as needed

Reach | Events and Community team

- Priority access to top-tier media and VCs at:
  - Six-plus Media Matchmaking Days
  - Four-plus VC Matchmaking Days
  - Ten-plus media dinners
- Exclusive invites to twenty-plus workshops focused on:
  - Narrative techniques
  - Awards and panel placements
  - Media training and more
- Creator engagement

- ◦ Seeding initial community
- ◦ Launch announcement(s), ongoing pitch strategy, draft messaging, etc.
- ◦ Creating new and ongoing engagement with Creator playbook
- STARTUP X–Hosted event curation, coordination, and strategy
  - ◦ BAM will support with one of the following initiatives per quarter with the option to pivot as priorities change
    - ▪ Bimonthly Community X Dinner
    - ▪ Quarterly Community X Workshop
    - ▪ Monthly Community X Webinar
  - ◦ BAM's support will include activities such as:
    - ▪ Monthly strategy session to identify new Slack community engagement techniques and initiatives
    - ▪ Event planning and coordination (venue comms, menu selection, day-of details)
    - ▪ Copy for invites to Community X
    - ▪ Prep for STARTUP X executive hosts
    - ▪ Attendee management and comms
    - ▪ Attendee follow-up strategy
    - ▪ Media invitations *(for fitting events)*
    - ▪ ROI reporting for each event
    - ▪ On-site support: *Travel and accommodation for up to two BAM team members will be sent for approval as an OOP cost per event*

Engage | BAM's CEO

- Inclusion in weekly and monthly email communications to VCs and LPs in the BAM network
- Quarterly VC engagement strategy session with CEO
- Investor deck strategy and feedback for STARTUP X

OPTION B: MEDIA RELATIONS AND EVENTS FOCUS, $18,000 PER MONTH

Media Relations

- Custom onboarding for goal, audience, and KPI alignment
- Quarterly comprehensive PR plan and tactical timeline
- Quarterly one-hour messaging review to sharpen STARTUP X's why, how, and what and hone competitive differentiation
- Two to three press releases over six months (e.g., launch announcement, Creator/EMR announcements)
- At least eight to ten media placements in national, business, tech, health tech, and relevant trade outlets
- Monthly proactive angle generation
- Monthly announcement coordination
- Ongoing newsjacking
- Ongoing reactive pitching
- Media preparedness (interview memos, interview prep)
- One news scan per week with up to four competitors
- Weekly meetings for real-time reporting and brainstorming
- Quarterly BAM Insights Reporting

Amplify | Marketing team

- Quarterly strategy session to define priorities and actions, which may include a mix of the deliverables listed below, in coordination with STARTUP X's in-house team that is currently creating and launching small content pieces over the next six months.
  - Drafted messaging and positioning for STARTUP X's EMR landing pages
  - Drafted PR and marketing playbook for Creators

Events and Community

- Priority access to top-tier media and VCs at:
  - Six-plus Media Matchmaking Days
  - Four-plus VC Matchmaking Days
  - Ten-plus media dinners
- Exclusive invites to twenty-plus workshops focused on:
  - Narrative techniques
  - Awards and panel placements
  - Media training and more
- Creator engagement
  - Assisting in initial community development
  - Launch announcement(s), ongoing pitch strategy, messaging support, etc.

HERE'S HOW WE'LL GET STARTED WORKING TOGETHER

We're in action mode from day one. Signing the MSA sets the wheels in motion and leads us to a collaborative Getting Started Meeting within the first ten days. Here, we lay the groundwork for success with key deliverables: a customized media list, a strategic PR plan, and a ninety-day timeline. We'll also set up a joint Slack channel to optimize communication.

As the calendar moves forward, so does our momentum. The thirty- and sixty-day marks are not mere checkpoints but strategic pivots where we fine-tune media relations, explore compelling story angles, and solidify media relationships.

And at the ninety-day mark? We're just getting started. We'll hold a comprehensive review that is both a celebration of success and a blueprint for the future, providing a clear path to the next stage of our relationship.

Our partnership is more than a series of actions; it's a commitment to your success. Strategic, dynamic, and forward-thinking, we're here to elevate your brand together.

YOUR COMMITMENT

- Main point of contact (CMO, Head of Marketing—someone who can make decisions)
  - Two to ten hours a week, depending on announcements
    - Daily conversations on Slack and email
    - Weekly thirty-minute Zoom calls
    - One-off calls/meetings as needed
    - Internal coordination for interviews/assets/data gathering
- CEO/Founder
  - Two to five hours a month, depending on announcements
    - Participation on at least two calls a month
    - Review of interview memos
    - Participation on quarterly reviews
    - Interviews with media
    - Media training and prep
    - Thought leadership development

HERE'S WHAT WE NEED FROM YOU TO BE SUCCESSFUL

BAM believes in partnership, one of our core values. We want to ensure you, as our client, are aligned with what partnership entails so we can do great work together. Below are promises we need you to agree to in order to make our partnership the best possible:

- I understand I need to participate in weekly or twice-a-month calls with BAM, give feedback during these calls, and, as much as feasible, do so in a direct and *Radical Candor* way. I understand I need to participate to the best of my ability in media facilitation, including being prepared for my media interviews, appearing on time, accepting that media will sometimes need last-minute access, and so on.

- I understand I need to work together with BAM to deliver materials, insights, data, commentary, and so on in order for media placements to be produced. I get that I just can't sit back, give BAM nothing, and expect top-tier press.

- I understand "media placements" include mentions, features, bylines, and various forms of "placements" that contribute to my KPIs and have reviewed BAM's FAQ doc that gives me dozens of samples and definitions. I get that not ALL my media placements will be full features because that is unreasonable.
  - **NOTE:** BAM will prioritize the previously discussed goal(s) when securing media placements for STARTUP X but cannot guarantee outcomes in top-tier or other outlets, considering the current media landscape.

- I understand if I decline a messaging workshop with BAM, I am responsible for giving BAM clear messaging guidelines that are shown on one to two pages at most and articulate STARTUP X's mission, "why," and distinctions.

- Ultimately, I understand and agree that if I am not a willing partner, the KPIs set above are likely to change, and BAM will proactively address this with me so we can find a solution. BAM may also terminate our relationship if I'm an unwilling partner.

- I am including the names of up to four competitors below so my team at BAM can actively track their activity. I will update my BAM team every quarter if this list changes so BAM is fully aware and can work with other clients that may be adjacent, but not direct competitors, to STARTUP X:

Competitor:
Competitor:
Competitor:
Competitor:

_____ (initial)

MASTER SERVICES AGREEMENT
STARTUP X

This master services agreement (the "Agreement") is effective as of the date listed on the signature page, hereto (the "Effective Date"), by and between BAM BY BIG LLC., doing business as BAM, XXX ("BAM"), and STARTUP X ("Client") located at XXX. BAM and Client are also referred to herein individually as a Party and collectively as the Parties.

SCOPE OF WORK

BAM will deliver (PR and/or Marketing) services as discussed in the presentation. Below are the expected deliverables for six months:

- TBD upon STARTUP X's scope selection

GENERAL TERMS

1. **SERVICES:** BAM will deliver (PR and Marketing) services as discussed in the presentation and in the scope of work from August 1, 2024–January 31, 2025.
   A. **PR and Media Relations:** $TBD per month
2. **PAYMENT AND BONUS:** Client acknowledges and expressly agrees to the duration of this Agreement (the "Term") and the compensation (the "Payment") as follows:
   A. **$TBD** per month starting August 1, 2024
   B. $750 admin fee per month. This "admin fee" covers all our PR tools and subscriptions, such as Muck Rack, Cision, mailing stuff to media, and more. This also means you don't get any itemized additional charges from us that are annoying. The admin fee doesn't include "big" expenses over $500 though, such as air travel or press release distributions via PR Newswire. For anything over $500, we will always get your approval in writing.
   C. **$TBD per month total to be invoiced**

The BAM team is a competitive, high-energy, and motivated team. As such, we now have a bonus structure in place to aim to delight our clients with above-and-beyond results. In addition to the monthly retainer above, Client will pay BAM a one-time fee of:

- Fifty percent of the retainer above ($TBD) every quarter if media-placement KPIs are exceeded by 5X.
- Media placement KPIs exceeding 5X a **quarter** equal: Y placements (X placements X 5). This applies to placements secured by BAM, not inbound opportunities that are sent directly to Client.
  ◦ With approval from Client, BAM will monitor and share bonus completion status.

Half of this bonus will go directly to Cient's team at BAM; the remainder will go to BAM overall, which includes the help of other BAM team members who achieve results collectively for Client.

Client will be invoiced monthly on the first day of each month. The initial payment, due upon the signing of the Agreement, will include the first month's services. Payment is due within fifteen days of invoice.

*If paid promotion (Twitter, LinkedIn, etc.) is included in services, Client must provide a credit card for all paid promotion costs. BAM will not be responsible for covering these costs up front.

Accounts Payable info for BAM's internal:

- Company legal name: **STARTUP X, Inc.**
- Client point person for Accounts Payable: _____
- Client point person for Accounts Payable's email: _____
- Client point person for Accounts Payable's phone number: _____
- Client point person for Accounts Payable's billing address: _____
- Initial invoice date: **August 1, 2024**
- Total invoice amount (Retainer + Admin Fee): **TBD**
- Bonus amount if obtained (must send verification to finance team): **TBD**
- Initial contract dates (Start–Stop): **August 1, 2024–January 31, 2025**
- Contract terms (if applicable, termination clause, any negotiated details relevant to contract terms go here): **Standard six-month contract**
- Product/Service (PR, Marketing, BAMx, Project, etc.): **TBD—Media Relations or CARE package**

3. **DELIVERY:** If BAM requires materials, content, information,

or any other items from Client for BAM to perform the services contemplated herein ("Client Deliverables"), Client acknowledges that any such Client Deliverables are due at least one week (five business days) prior to utilization by BAM. Client's failure to submit required Client Deliverables may cause delays in delivery of BAM's services with no penalty to BAM.

BAM's services are deemed complete upon delivery to Client or upon Client approval if indicated as a project pending approval by BAM.

4. **ESTIMATED DELIVERY DATES:** Delivery of the services shall mean delivery by BAM as described in the BAM Proposal. Client understands and acknowledges that the Estimated Delivery Dates are mere estimates and are not guaranteed. Additionally, Client understands that any changes to the BAM Proposal after execution of this Agreement may result in delays to the Estimated Delivery Dates.

5. **CHANGE ORDERS:** Client expressly agrees to make a reasonable attempt to notify BAM as soon as practicable if it wishes to change any details that are described in the BAM Proposal. If such changes result in additional costs to BAM, BAM agrees to notify Client of the amount before any such additional costs are incurred, and BAM shall proceed only after receiving approval (written or oral) from Client. Approval by Client shall be binding and incorporated into the terms of this Agreement. Reimbursement for such additional costs shall be payable in accordance with the terms of this Agreement for final payment.

6. **REPORTING:** BAM will retain accurate records of all costs incurred on Client's behalf and will be prepared to supply any supporting detail required by Client's auditors and desig-

nated representatives. BAM will meet bimonthly with Client to review tasks and progress. In addition, an hours allocation can be presented, if requested by Client, so that Client can view utilization of the monthly budget.

7. **POINT OF CONTACT:** Client will designate one individual as the Point of Contact, and BAM will only accept critiques and changes regarding the services from that person. Client understands and agrees that any requests and/or information from an individual that is not the Point of Contact will not be included. BAM will not be held responsible if Client is not satisfied with the final product due to information disseminated to BAM by any individual other than the Point of Contact.

8. **INTELLECTUAL PROPERTY THAT YOU OWN:** Client understands and expressly agrees that the rights and ownership granted in the services, if any, are hereby withheld from Client until Client makes full payment for the Term of this Agreement. Upon full Payment, the following shall take effect:

Client and BAM agree that the services, and related media and/or assets, TO BE DELIVERED BY BAM, and any proceeds thereof, constitute a work made for hire pursuant to Section 101(2) of the United States Copyright Act of 1976. Accordingly, CLIENT WILL BE THE OWNER of the copyright, patent, trademark, and any other intellectual property rights in the proceeds. BAM hereby assigns to Client, to the extent that the work-for-hire provisions of the US and foreign copyright laws do not apply, all BAM's title and ownership interest in any copyright and any other intellectual property rights throughout the universe covering the proceeds from the services. Client may register the copyright, patent, trademark, and otherwise protect its interest in the rights granted herein in its own name. BAM will cooperate with Client, at Client's expense, as necessary to perfect Client's rights in the proceeds as provided herein. All Projects must be attributed to BAM when used publicly.

9. **OUR PRE-EXISTING MATERIALS THAT WE OWN:** All rights not expressly granted above are reserved to BAM, including but not limited to all rights to sketches, comps, or other preliminary materials created by BAM. BAM is not permitted to disclose ANY materials given by Client. For the sake of clarity, this section contemplates preexisting materials and intellectual property independently developed by BAM and shall remain the exclusive property of BAM; any of these materials used in the services delivered to Client shall be provided to Client as a license for use as contemplated by this Agreement but remain the property of BAM.

10. **PERFORMANCE:** BAM shall make best efforts to produce successful results from BAM's services for Client, but BAM makes no representations, guarantees, or warranties as to the effectiveness or performance of the services delivered, with the exception of Section 13 below.

11. **SATISFACTION:** The obligation of Client to make Payment to BAM according to the terms of this Agreement is not conditioned on Client's satisfaction with the proceeds of services under this Agreement, so long as Client and BAM communicated throughout BAM's provision of services and Client did not express dissatisfaction with final deliverables or services. As such, the Payment due under this Agreement is in consideration of the provision of services by BAM and not in consideration of the return or effectiveness of BAM's services. Client understands and expressly agrees that delivery of the services under this Agreement shall obligate Client to make Payment and Payment shall not be withheld due to dissatisfaction with the results of those services.

12. **BAM FEES:** BAM shall be entitled to apply an inflationary increase in Fees on each twelve-month anniversary date ("Anniversary Date") after the commencement of this Contract. Any fee uplift will be the increase in the Consumer Prices Index ("CPI") (or a similar inflation index for the above market if the CPI does not exist) for the period concerned. The increased Fees shall take effect from, or within a reasonable period of, the Anniversary Date.

13. **NONEXCLUSIVE:** This Agreement is nonexclusive. BAM is free to provide services to other parties during the Term of this Agreement, provided that such provision of services to others does not materially interfere with the terms and obligations of this Agreement. For the sake of clarity, BAM endeavors to evaluate every opportunity presented to it to ensure that no conflict of interest would arise by taking on said opportunities, and in the event that BAM perceives a potential conflict with a competing business, BAM will promptly discuss with Client in advance of working with said potentially competitive business.

14. **EMPLOYMENT OF OTHERS:** The Client may from time to time request that BAM arrange for the services of others. The Client will pay all costs to BAM for the services of parties requested by Client. Additionally, BAM may employ the services of other independent contractors or service providers without the permission of Client in order to complete the services. BAM shall be responsible for supervision and control of any employees or independent contractors who perform services pursuant to this Agreement. All such persons shall be employees and/or contractors of BAM and not of Client. The responsibility for specification of the work to be performed and the specific services hereunder shall be exclusively that of BAM.

15. **CONFIDENTIALITY AND SAFEGUARD OF PROPERTY:** Client and BAM acknowledge that in connection with this

Agreement, they may have occasion to receive or review certain confidential or proprietary technical and business information and materials of the other party. Client and BAM, as well as their agents and employees, respectively agree to keep in confidence and not to disclose or use for its own respective benefit or for the benefit of any third party (except as may be required for the performance of services under this Agreement or as may be required by law) any information, documents, or materials that are reasonably considered confidential regarding each other's products, business, customers, clients, suppliers, or methods of operation, provided, however, that such obligation of confidentiality will not extend to anything in the public domain or that was in the possession of either Party prior to disclosure. BAM and Client will take reasonable precautions to safeguard property of the other entrusted to it, but in the absence of negligence or willful disregard, neither BAM nor Client will be responsible for any loss or damage.

16. **PROMOTION:** Client grants the right to BAM and BAM may use Client's name and company information in all advertising and promotional material, including via social media. Additionally, Client may publish or disclose information regarding the services contemplated by this Agreement and shall acknowledge the support of BAM in all such publications. Client may disclose and publish the support BAM provides to Client, so long as Client notifies BAM and receives approval in advance for such publication or disclosure.

17. **INDEPENDENT CONTRACTOR:** The relationship of the Parties under this Agreement is one of independent contractors, and no joint venture, partnership, agency, employer-employee, or similar relationship is created by this Agreement or the Parties' related conduct. BAM has the sole right to control and direct the means, details, manner, and method by which the

services will be completed. BAM shall complete the services, and Client is not required to hire, supervise, or pay any assistants to help BAM. Accordingly, BAM shall be responsible for payment of all taxes, including federal, state, and local taxes, arising out of BAM's activities in accordance with this Agreement, including by way of illustration but not limitation federal and state income tax, Social Security tax, Unemployment Insurance taxes, and any other taxes or business license fee as required. As such, the amount of time devoted to Client by BAM shall be adequate to complete the services, as identified by the BAM Proposal, but the amount of time may vary from day to day or week to week at BAM's discretion.

18. **STARTUP X VERIFICATION:** Client understands and expressly agrees that it is Client's sole responsibility to ensure the accuracy, completeness, and legality of any content and/or information provided to BAM. It is hereby understood that BAM cannot undertake to verify facts supplied by Client or factual matters included in material prepared by BAM and approved in writing by Client. Client agrees to indemnify and hold harmless BAM from and against any and all losses, claims, damages, expenses (including reasonable legal expenses), or liabilities that BAM may incur (a) based upon information, representations, reports, data, or releases furnished or approved by Client or Client's representatives for use or release by BAM, whether or not BAM prepares or participates in the preparation in such material, and (b) resulting from any and all actions performed by BAM and/or its agents at the request of Client. In the event that BAM's actions or conduct in performance of this Agreement gives rise to losses, claims, damages, expenses (including reasonable legal expenses), or liabilities attributable to BAM's negligence, willful misconduct, or violation of law, BAM shall indemnify and hold Client harmless for such

losses, claims, damages, expenses (including reasonable legal expenses), or liabilities directly attributable to BAM's negligence, willful misconduct, or violation of law.

19. **ASSIGNMENT:** BAM reserves the right to assign the services to other designers or subcontractors to ensure quality and on-time completion. Client may not resell, assign, or transfer any of its rights or obligations hereunder, and any attempt to resell, assign, or transfer such rights or obligations will be null and void without BAM's prior written approval.

20. **ENTIRE AGREEMENT:** This Agreement will constitute the entire agreement of the Parties with respect to the subject matter hereof and supersede all previous communications, representations, understandings, and agreements, either oral or written, between the Parties with respect to the subject matter of this Agreement. The Agreement may be executed in counterparts, each of which will be an original and all of which together will constitute one and the same document. No modification of these Terms will be binding unless in writing and signed by both Parties. If any provision herein is held to be unenforceable, the remaining provisions will remain in full force and effect. All rights and remedies hereunder are cumulative.

21. **SEVERABILITY AND NON-WAIVER:** If any provision of this Agreement is held in whole or in part to be unenforceable for any reason, the remainder of that provision and of the entire Agreement will be severable and remain in effect. Any failure by BAM to require Client's performance of any provision in this Agreement shall not affect BAM's right to require performance at any time thereafter, nor shall a waiver of any breach or default of this Agreement constitute a waiver of any subsequent breach or default or a waiver of the provision itself.

22. **TERMINATION:** The Term of this Contract shall be for a min-

imum period of six (6) months commencing on August 1, 2024. During the initial Term, the notice period is thirty days and may be given within the last thirty days of the term. This Contract cannot be terminated sooner than the last thirty days of the initial six months. If no notice is given, BAM will operate on a rolling thirty-day notice period at a $XX a month budget until otherwise revised in writing. Client must give BAM written notice of termination anytime beyond January 31, 2025.

In the event that the services are postponed or terminated at the request of Client, BAM shall have the right to bill pro rata for work completed through the date of that request while reserving all rights under this Agreement. If additional payment is due, it shall be payable within thirty (30) days of Client's written notice of termination. Client shall also pay any expenses incurred by BAM, and BAM shall own all rights to the services. Client shall assume responsibility for all legal fees necessitated by default in payment. In the event of a material breach of this Agreement by Client, all remaining Payments shall be immediately due and payable and BAM shall have no obligation to perform any further services.

23. **FORCE MAJEURE:** BAM shall not be deemed in breach of this Agreement if BAM is unable to complete the services or any portion thereof by reason of fire, earthquake, labor dispute, act of a public enemy, death, illness, or incapacity of BAM or any local, state, federal, national, or international law; governmental order or regulation; or any other event beyond BAM's control (collectively "Force Majeure Events"). Upon occurrence of any Force Majeure Event, BAM shall give notice to Client of its inability to perform or of delay in completing services and shall propose revisions to the schedule for completion of the services.

24. **GOVERNING LAW:** This Agreement will be governed by the laws of the State of California. Client and BAM agree that any claims, legal proceedings, or litigation arising in connection with this Agreement will be brought solely in the courts of the County of San Diego, and the Parties consent to the jurisdiction of such courts. If any claim of dispute arising out of, or relating to, this Agreement is not settled promptly in the ordinary course of business, the Parties shall seek to resolve such dispute between them, first, by negotiating promptly in good faith. If the Parties are unable to resolve the dispute within twenty (20) business days (or such period as the Parties otherwise agree), then any such dispute shall be resolved by binding arbitration conducted by a single arbitrator under the rules of the American Arbitration Association at a mutually agreed upon location. The arbitrator must base his or her decision upon this Agreement and applicable law. If any legal action is necessary to enforce this Agreement, the prevailing Party shall be entitled to reasonable attorney fees, costs, and expenses.

25. **NON-SOLICITATION:** During this Agreement and for a period of twelve (12) months following the termination of this Agreement, each Party shall refrain from soliciting for employment or otherwise any employee of the other Party or independent contractor who exclusively provides services to the other Party or induce or otherwise advise any such employee or independent contractor of the other Party to leave the employment of the other Party. In the event that a Party does solicit, whether as an employee or independent contractor, an employee or independent contractor of the other Party during or within one (1) year following the termination of this Agreement, the hiring/retaining Party shall pay to the non-hiring/retaining Party a fee equal to one hundred percent (100%) of the employee or independent contractor's annual wage or rate (the "Placement

Fee"). The Placement Fee must be paid within fifteen (15) days of the date of such hiring/retention.

26. **DEI EFFORTS:** Effective January 1, 2021, all BAM clients not already actively engaging in Diversity, Equity, and Inclusion ("DEI") training are encouraged to implement some level of DEI initiative and/or training. BAM will not dictate specifics of the DEI initiative/training. The specifics of the DEI training/initiative will be of Client's discretion. BAM is able to provide Client with resources, guidance, and continued support from BAM's Head of People. Here is a direct link to the initial resources provided.

This proposal will remain open until the close of business on July 19, 2024. To indicate your acceptance of the terms and conditions set forth in this letter, please sign and date this document as referenced below.

IN WITNESS WHEREOF, BAM and STARTUP X have executed this Agreement:

BAM	STARTUP X
Name: Rebecca Bamberger	Name:
Title: Chief Executive Officer	Title:
Signature:	Signature:
Date:	Date:

BLOG POST RELATED TO ROUNDS OF FUNDING AND BAM'S WORK

2023 UPDATE: BAM'S VENTURE-BACKED CLIENTS RAISE 94 PERCENT MORE FUNDING

A 2023 update to BAM's speed-to-funding research:

Last year, BAM partnered with Stitch, an independent third-party marketing research firm, to evaluate our clients' fundraising results versus the market at large. The original results showed that BAM clients raise 107 percent more funding than the average VC-backed tech company.

Twelve months later, the market is *very* different. According to a Crunchbase report, Q3 2022 venture funding was down 53 percent year-over-year, and fewer companies are joining the unicorn club. **Despite these headwinds, the 2023 update on our Stitch report showed that BAM clients raise 94 percent more funding than the average VC-backed tech company.**

Similar to last year's report, BAM clients, on average, took longer to receive funding than the Crunchbase sample. But this year's update shows that BAM clients raised faster than last year. There were fewer days between raising rounds one and two and rounds two and three for BAM clients compared to BAM clients last year. Overall, BAM clients raised a total of 94 percent more funding than other venture-backed startups:

- BAM clients raised 46 percent more than the average venture-backed tech company for funding round one
- Fourteen percent less for funding round two
- One hundred one percent more for funding round three
- One hundred two percent more for funding round four

We're proud to see that the data backs up what we already anecdotally know to be true: Our clients raise! Do you want to experience the BAM effect for your startup? Let's get to work!

Original 2022 data:

Stitch, a third-party marketing research firm, has confirmed BAM clients raise 107 percent more funding than the average VC-backed tech company.

To calculate this metric, Stitch sampled three hundred companies from Crunchbase's database, filtered by industry—artificial intelligence, healthcare technologies, cybersecurity, and cloud security—and funding round to match BAM clients' 2016 to 2022 funding rounds.

Stitch then compared the sample set with BAM clients from 2016 to 2022. The results showed that while BAM clients took on average 22 percent longer between funding rounds, they raised more money. In particular:

- BAM clients raised 53 percent more than the average venture-backed tech company for Series A funding
- Sixty-four percent more for Series B
- One hundred percent more for Series C
- Two hundred fifty-one percent more for Series D
- One hundred seven percent more for the total funding amount

"This five-year-span study gives us quantitative data that backs up what we've felt and known for a long time: The storytelling we do for our clients and our vast network of venture capitalists means serious money."

—BAM CEO, BECK BAMBERGER

Data is a key aspect of our storytelling, and we're proud of what this data now confirms: BAM clients overwhelmingly raise more money than other startups.

Even with a comparative dip in average Round 2 funding, BAM clients' rounds of funding *accelerated to higher levels* than the Crunchbase sample. As in 2022, the later the round, the more of a difference BAM makes.

2023 UPDATE

Client Group	Average Amount of Round 1 Funding	Average Amount of Round 2 Funding	Average Amount of Round 3 Funding	Average Amount of Round 4 Funding
BAM*	$13.9M +46%	$18.3M -14%	$47.8M +101%	$48.7M +102%
Crunchbase Sample	$9.5M	$21.3M	$23.8M	$24.1M

2022

Client Group	Average Amount of Round 1 Funding	Average Amount of Round 2 Funding	Average Amount of Round 3 Funding	Average Amount of Round 4 Funding
BAM*	$15.3M +53%	$34.5M +64%	$42.0M +100%	$98.0M +251%
Crunchbase Sample	$10.0M	$21.0M	$21.1M	$27.9M

PRESS RELEASE SAMPLE

THOMVEST VENTURES ANNOUNCES NEW $250M FUND AND PROMOTES TWO TO LEADERSHIP TEAM

SF-based venture capital fund Thomvest Ventures increases its total assets under management to $750M and promotes Umesh Padval and Nima Wedlake to Managing Directors.

SAN FRANCISCO, Jan. 16, 2024/PRNewswire/—**Thomvest Ventures**, a venture capital firm founded by Peter Thomson, today announced a new $250 million fund and the promotion of Umesh

Padval and Nima Wedlake to the role of Managing Director. The new fund brings the firm's total assets under management (AUM) to $750 million, enabling the firm to invest in the next generation of companies across the firm's core focus areas of financial and real estate technology, cybersecurity, cloud, and AI infrastructure.

"I started investing in entrepreneurs because of their potential to help shape our collective future," said Peter Thomson, founder of Thomvest Ventures. "We believe that great companies are often born during challenging macroeconomic periods. And given the once-in-a-generation changes that we see happening now because of AI, that potential is as strong today as ever."

Founded more than twenty-five years ago, Thomvest Ventures has made over seventy-five investments across early- and growth-stage startups. Notable investments have included Blend Labs, Carta, Clari, Cohere, Cylance, Harness.io, Kabbage, Isovalent, Ladder, LendingClub, Mynd, SoFi, Skyhigh Networks, ThousandEyes, and Vungle. The firm's stage-agnostic, sector-specific approach is driven by its ongoing market research efforts and extensive operator and advisor network.

Don Butler, the firm's current Managing Director, said, "Our experience of investing over the last quarter century means that we've lived through several market cycles. The combination of the current downturn in venture and the opportunities that AI enables make this the right time to be investing in the next generation of leaders in our focus areas."

As part of the new fund, Thomvest Ventures is also announcing the promotion of two investors, Umesh Padval and Nima Wedlake, to the role of Managing Director. The two partners bring significant experience and an impressive investment track record to their respective areas.

Umesh Padval leads the firm's investments in cybersecurity, cloud, and AI infrastructure. Umesh has led Thomvest Ventures investments in a number of fast-growing companies, including Bolster, Cohere, Clari, Cycognito, Harness.io, Isovalent (acquired by Cisco), Lastline (acquired by VMWare), Skyhigh Networks (acquired by McAfee), and ThousandEyes (acquired by Cisco).

"The disruption caused by generative AI this year provides us with a tremendous opportunity to create the next generation of companies in cybersecurity, cloud, and AI infrastructure," said Umesh Padval. "Our firm has been investing in companies that leverage AI for years like Bolster, Clari, Cylance, Harness, and Qwiet AI, and our latest investment in Cohere marks our first in generative AI. We are humbled by the trust and confidence placed on us by founders and CEOs who have chosen to partner with us to build large enterprises. Our CEO and extensive board experience, combined with our CXO network, operational expertise, and the deep knowledge of the verticals we invest in, significantly differentiates us in the start-up community."

Nima Wedlake leads the firm's investments in real estate technology. Nima has led the firm's investment in a number of current and emerging industry leaders, including Baselane, Blend, Keyway, Maxwell, Mynd, and Obie.

"We continue to see a number of unique opportunities in real estate—we are in the early days of digital transformation within the asset class," said Nima. "I'm thrilled to be able to leverage our deep understanding of the space to support transformational founders and management teams."

ABOUT THOMVEST VENTURES

Thomvest Ventures is a venture capital fund backed by Peter Thomson. The firm is focused on financial and property technology, cybersecurity, and cloud and AI infrastructure. Thomvest Ventures has been investing in entrepreneurs for more than twenty-five years through its offices in Silicon Valley and Toronto. The firm is committed to helping our companies become leaders in their fields through leveraging our industry expertise and company-building experience. To learn more about Thomvest Ventures, please visit: **https://www.thomvest.com/**

PRESS RELEASE SAMPLE
ARTA FINANCE OFFICIALLY OPENS TO ALL QUALIFIED INVESTORS, ANNOUNCES $100 MILLION IN MEMBER ASSETS

NEWS PROVIDED BY ARTA FINANCE

After being in invite-only mode and refining the product with early members, Arta Finance reaches milestone in member assets, hires industry leaders, and launches new AI-driven services to enable access to the same investments as the ultra-wealthy.

MOUNTAIN VIEW, Calif., Oct. 18, 2023/PRNewswire/—**Arta Finance**, a fintech company transforming the way people grow, protect, and enjoy their wealth, today announced it has officially opened its digital family office platform to all qualified investors in the US. Arta came out of stealth in late 2022 after raising over $90 million and started onboarding members through an invite-only program earlier this year. Since then, Arta has significantly expanded its product offering and hired industry leaders to scale the platform in the US and beyond. Members have trusted Arta to manage more than $100 million on their behalf and are deepening their engagement with the platform to create better financial futures for themselves and their families.

The assets of America's top 1 percent have skyrocketed from the second quarter of 2020 to 2023, mainly driven by strong returns on investments from stocks and other assets. Over this three-year period, the investments of the top 1 percent outperformed the remaining population by about 30 percent, according to data from the Federal Reserve. The increasing divide in wealth indicates continued inequality in wealth-generating opportunities—what Arta terms the "financial superpowers"—for the vast majority of people. Arta Finance addresses this by providing access to investment opportunities and financial strategies typically only available to the ultra-wealthy via family offices and private banks. Arta makes these available by setting up a digital family office for each of its members, applying the latest in artificial intelligence technology, and customizing support to help members build their financial futures.

"The excitement and trust our members have shown has been incredible. We knew that many professionals felt this opportunity gap when it came to making their money work for them, including the founding team. Since Arta started accepting members, it's become even more clear that a digital family office is filling an unmet need as professionals, busy with their careers and families, look for ways to expand beyond basic ETFs, robo-advisors, and 401(k) plans. We have seen a lot of interest in navigating today's volatile, high-interest-rate environment; getting access to alternative investments; and leveraging other 'financial superpowers' of the ultra-wealthy," said Caesar Sengupta, co-founder and CEO of

Arta Finance. "Arta's members are embracing the use of AI in their personal digital family offices, and with our most recent features and services, Arta is ready to help even more people gain access to the same powerful resources as the ultra-wealthy."

Over the past year, Arta's member base has grown from employees at firms like Apple, Google, Microsoft, and Stripe— from first-time investors to financial sophisticates. All these members are looking to grow, protect, and enjoy their wealth as the ultra-wealthy do. Today, Arta is proud to announce the following new services and features to deliver on the digital family office promise:

- Growing Wealth
  - Private Market Access: Members now have access to an expanded selection of private equity, private credit, and real estate investments from top-tier private investors like Vista, TPG, Nuveen, and more. Arta is also introducing Venture Capital as an investment class for qualified members.
  - Customized Public Market Investments with AI: Later this quarter, Arta will introduce Arta Copilot to leverage Large Language Models (LLMs) for the creation, research, and management of highly customized AMPs (AI-Managed Portfolios). Arta's Defensive Growth AMPs will also expand to enable customization by sectors, geography, and additional risk controls.
  - Principal Protected Growth: An investment product that enables members to capture a majority of US stock market growth while protecting their initial investment. Structured products like this are typically available only to the ultra-rich through their private banks.
- Protecting Wealth
  - Weathgen Insurance: Members can now leverage this

"financial superpower" that is used by the ultra-wealthy to grow and transfer wealth in a tax-advantaged manner using Permanent Life Insurance policies.

- Tax and Estate Planning Services: Members can meet with a certified expert who will help protect their loved ones and preserve their wealth while minimizing income, gift, and estate taxes.
- Tax Loss Harvesting: Arta will be introducing automated tax-loss harvesting later this quarter to ensure more returns earned make it back into the hands of members.

• Enjoying Wealth
- Personal Assistant Services: Access to virtual personal assistants who can help members supercharge their efficiency and take back control of their time.
- Connecting with Others: Through online and in-person opportunities, members are able to connect with finance and investment experts to learn, benchmark, and inspire each other.

In addition to these services and features, Tomas Arlia was hired as Head of Private Markets to expand access, reduce complexity, and develop capital availability for private-market investments. Prior to joining Arta Finance, Arlia oversaw a $3 billion global hedge fund and $1 billion portfolio in private-equity-fund investments as the Chief Investment Officer at GE Asset Management. In addition to Arlia, David Oh was hired as the Head of Tax and Estate Planning to support members with wealth transfer and tax solutions for preserving generational family wealth. Before joining Arta, Oh was the Managing Director and Trust Counsel at Fiduciary Trust International and Director of Tax and Estate Planning at Charles Schwab. Arlia and Oh join Arta's Head of Insurance, Samita Malik, who joined Arta after spending two decades building insurance products at Aegon Insurance, MetLife, Aviva, and Bain.

"Hiring experts from different sectors of finance to provide a comprehensive digital family office has proven to be extremely beneficial to our members. They can leverage the deep domain expertise these experts bring but at much lower costs and enjoy a better user experience via our digital platform," said Sengupta. "This past year, our team nearly doubled in size, and we plan to bring on more industry leaders in 2024 to help us democratize private banking, family office services, and grow our presence globally."

Arta Finance is currently available to individuals who meet the SEC definition of Accredited Investor, Qualified Purchaser, or Qualified Client. Arta's long-term goal is to expand access to everyone. To learn more about Arta Finance, please visit www.artafinance.com.

See important disclosures here.

ABOUT ARTA FINANCE

Arta Finance is the digital family office for the world. It empowers more people to gain the financial superpowers that, until now, were the exclusive domain of ultra-high-net-worth individuals. Arta Finance, a US SEC-registered investment advisor, harnesses AI and machine learning to enable intelligent investing in public-market equities, provides access to alternative investments—including private equity, venture capital, and real-estate—and connects members to financial expertise so they can advance their unique goals. Founded by a team of former Google executives, Arta is backed by Sequoia Capital India, Ribbit Capital, Coatue, and more than 140 luminaries in tech and finance. To learn more about Arta, visit artafinance.com.

Acknowledgments

———

This book wouldn't exist if it weren't for the sheer power and commitment of my team at BAM, the agency I founded years ago. Media relations is a team sport, and there is no one I'd rather be playing the game with than those at BAM, who have been on this grand adventure with me for years and now decades. We're a very serious company, after all.

In addition, I want to shout out to the community of comms and marketing heads at venture capital funds who have supported BAM throughout the years. This book was spurred from several conversations I had with so many great PR folks in the VC comms and marketing community who agreed PR and marketing resources for venture-backed founders were lacking. Lastly, I deeply appreciate the hundreds of venture-backed founders we've had the honor of working with. You gave us your babies (your startups), blessing us to craft your stories to the media, which is an exercise in trust and faith. The venture capital world is wild, and the media one is savage, as you know. Thank you for being true partners with us.